Praise for GPS for Success: Skills, Strategies, and Secrets of Superachievers

Dr. Barry Franklin's book is an exceptional guide for anyone who aspires to career advancement. Dr. Franklin has unraveled the secrets of the most successful people from every field. This book provides step-by-step instructions that each of us can follow. He proves that goal-setting, persistence, hard work, and kindness will enable ordinary people to achieve extraordinary results. Dr. Franklin's own career is a perfect example that his formula for success works—it is quite an inspiration!

—Ora Hirsch Pescovitz, MD, President, Oakland University

This down-to-earth treasure chest, disguised as a book, provides invaluable insights—whether you are just launching your career or are well on the way. Inspired by his colleague's dog Gus, Dr. Franklin identifies the values of giving beyond self, and of humility, preparation, resilience, and compassion. These values, coupled with a relentless and optimistic work ethic, will fuel a consequential life.

—Timothy P. White, PhD, Chancellor Emeritus and Professor, The California State University

GPS for Success is bursting with pearls of wisdom perfect for new grads just starting down the career path and for anyone in need of an energizing nudge toward taking the "yellow brick road" to achievement. Dr. Barry Franklin has woven together experiences and essentials from the world's most successful people and valued resources to inspire success, happiness, and personal fulfillment.

—Marjory Abrams, Former Executive Vice President and Chief Content Officer, Bottom Line Inc.

Dr. Barry Franklin has written a marvelous book that offers what we all can use: a blueprint for successful living. His research is first rate, his recommendations are practical, doable, and make great sense. Best of all, they work! *GPS for Success* delivers on its promise to provide skills, strategies, and secrets for building a successful life. It is a must-read for anyone wanting to live the life they imagine.

—**Joseph C. Piscatella, author** *Don't Eat Your Heart Out*

This high-energy power packed guide has the altimeter reading at the limit for Dr. Barry Franklin who is in the captain's seat. Having known Dr. Franklin for nearly three decades, his positivity and gusto for life embody an ever-accelerating rocket ship destined for a happier and more satisfied world. In this book, the positivity, enthusiasm, humility, respectfulness, circumspection, and assiduousness of a quintessential professional is fully developed. The messages and quick points are tacking for globals, millennials, Generation X, Generation Y, and young boomers. The reader will be buoyed by sage advice that is written and lived by one of America's leading motivational authors. Sit back, strap in, and countdown to success!

—**Peter A. McCullough, MD, MPH, Chief Medical Advisor, Truth for Health Foundation**

GPS for Success is a powerful, stimulating, and inspirational read! This book reveals what many people at the height of their profession have taken a lifetime to learn. It should be at the top of the list of required reading for anyone aspiring to a successful career!

—**Debra K. Brede, Founder D.K. Brede Investment Management Co.**

Dr. Franklin has adeptly described proactive, impactful, and transformational behaviors found in highly successful people. You will recognize characteristics that you have admired, including happiness, loving what you do, and serving others, and be challenged to develop outstanding people and communications skills that will positively influence your approach to life and ultimately your career path. *GPS for Success* is a must read.

—**Kathy Berra, MSN, NP-BC, Co-Director, The LifeCare Company, Clinical Trial Coordinator, Stanford Prevention Research Center (Ret)**

GPS for Success was written for the entry professional, but can also serve as a guiding light for those later in their careers looking to switch tracks, get out of a rut, or try to make the leap to the next level. The ideas of goal setting and visualization particularly resonate, as those consistently show up at the top of lists of those who are most successful. Dr. Franklin's ability to pull together tips, quotes, ideas, concepts, and challenges is unsurpassed. Ultimately, *GPS for Success* should be on the bookshelf of anyone who wants to be successful in life!

—Gary Liguori, PhD, Dean, College of Health Sciences, Professor, Department of Kinesiology, University of Rhode Island, Kingston, RI

GPS for Success is a book I have always wanted to read. And now, at last, it's been written. GPS is a unique and invaluable guide to life, success, and fulfillment. It should become part of everyone's road map to an extraordinary future.

—James R. Whitehead, CEO, International Society for Sports Psychiatry

This unique book details how ordinary people became leaders and winners in life. The traits, qualities, characteristics, and behaviors that empower individuals to perform at the highest levels of their professions are brought to light in an easy reading style that makes the book difficult to put down. Dr. Franklin has identified the key behavioral skills and methods of highly successful people in all walks of life and presented the material in a format that resonates with the reader. A must read for those wanting to climb the career ladder of success.

—Jeffrey A. Potteiger, PhD, Dean, Graduate School, Research Integrity Officer, Grand Valley State University

Having witnessed, firsthand, Dr. Franklin's presentation of this material to our students at Central Michigan University, I'm delighted that he has chronicled his life's experiences and career advice into an invaluable resource. Dr. Franklin's book is a must read for all students as it will help them succeed, not only in the classroom, but more importantly, in life.

—Thomas J. Masterson, Jr., PhD, Dean and Professor, The Herbert H. and Grace A. Dow College of Health Professions, Central Michigan University

Barry Franklin leaves no stone unturned when evaluating the relevant literature, pertinent quotations, and behavioral skills and strategies for maximizing professional success. The lessons conveyed are creatively woven together with inspirational, true stories into a helpful and easy-to-read book.

—Lori Ploutz-Snyder, PhD, Dean of the School of Kinesiology, University of Michigan

GPS for Success

GPS for Success

Skills, Strategies, and Secrets of Superachievers

By

Barry A. Franklin

with a Foreword by Mark Sanborn

Routledge
Taylor & Francis Group

A PRODUCTIVITY PRESS BOOK

First published 2022
by Routledge
605 Third Avenue, New York, NY 10158

and by Routledge
2 Park Square, Milton Park, Abingdon, Oxon, OX14 4RN

Routledge is an imprint of the Taylor & Francis Group, an informa business

Library of Congress Cataloging-in-Publication Data
A catalog record for this title has been requested

ISBN: 9781032196978 (hbk)
ISBN: 9781032196954 (pbk)
ISBN: 9781003260387 (ebk)

DOI: 10.4324/9781003260387

Typeset in Minion
by Deanta Global Publishing Services, Chennai, India

WARNING!

Reading this book and embracing the skills, strategies, and secrets contained herein, from many of the "superachievers" on our planet, past and present, will provide you with proven, practical, and priceless recommendations for future career success. Believe, act, achieve. By following these time-tested principles, *good luck* will be increasingly attracted to you. Unexpected opportunities will arise, and your breakthrough goals will come to fruition. It will happen! It cannot be otherwise. Don't be surprised. *GPS for Success* will empower you to live the life that you imagine. Buckle up and enjoy the exciting journey ahead. ☺

Perhaps renowned scientist Sir Isaac Newton summed it up best when he said, "If I have seen further, it is by standing on the shoulders of giants."

This book is dedicated to the Superachievers, past, present, and future, many of whom are described herein, whose behaviors, focus, and approach to life challenges and opportunities provide a blueprint for happiness and extraordinary career success.

To my wife Linda; son Michael; daughter Laura; their spouses, Carissa and Seth; and my grandchildren, Ethan, Liam, Samarah, and Schoen— the loves of my life. I can envision many things, but not a better family.

Contents

SECTION IV   Appendices

Foreword

I've met many people but only a few who have told me their hobby was studying highly successful people.

Barry Franklin is one of those people.

Highly successful in his own right, Barry leads a busy professional life in medicine and healthcare. He's obviously practiced what he's learned from his study of success.

In writing this book, Barry has done these three things for you:

He did the work. If you haven't made the time for study, Barry did it for you by focusing on how high performers achieve success.

He saved you time. You are busy. I am busy. We're all busy. By providing the distillation of what he's learned, Barry has saved you hundreds of hours.

He provides ideas you can use to be more successful. He doesn't just share what he's learned, but how you can apply the information in your business and life.

You'll learn the power of focusing on the significant few, why you should give people more than they expect, how to be just a little bit better and benefit from that improvement, and much more.

Here's how I suggest you use this compendium:

Highlight and take notes. Highlighting ideas lets you review them later, and taking notes aids in comprehension and retention.

Turn your favorite quotations into application. Quotes are the wisdom soundbites of our time, and this book is full of them. Rather than read them quickly and move on, contemplate the true meaning and how you can use it in your life.

Focus more on application than on simply interesting. You might find a story or idea that is interesting, or even inspiring, but it won't count for much if you don't figure out how to apply it.

Don't take shortcuts. When you come to an exercise or question, don't skip over it. By doing the work and answering the question, you'll get maximum benefit.

Share what you learn with others. Your family members, friends, and colleagues will benefit if you pass on the best ideas you run across. Sharing or teaching something also helps you remember it.

Write your own lessons. For the highly motivated, write your own work, whether an article or a book. Use this book as a springboard for success 2.0 and go from emulating successful achievers to becoming one.

BETTER QUESTIONS GET BETTER RESULTS

As you read Barry's work, you can frame what you learn using these questions:

1. What are you going to say "no" to?
2. What is the most important thing you need to learn or learn better?
3. What habitual time waster will you eliminate?
4. Which relationships, personal and professional, will you focus on improving?
5. What one thing will you do extraordinarily well to create the greatest success in your work?

Reading whatever we want and whenever we want is a gift that even today isn't available to all in the world. Being able to read doesn't count if you don't read. I believe that the cumulative IQ of our society will increase as more people exercise their right to read. Reading is central to self-education and lifelong learning, and if books have the power to save an individual, maybe they have the power to save a society as well.

Mark Sanborn, CSP, CPAE
President, Sanborn & Associates, Inc.
Author of The Fred Factor and You Don't Need a Title to Be a Leader

A Favorite Story

GPS. Global Positioning System. A navigation tool that gets people where they want to go, right? For me, GPS stands for Gus' Positioning System. Gus was one of our beloved Yellow Labrador Retrievers. With four dogs and two humans all wanting to sleep in the bed and sit on the furniture, things could get, let's say, competitive for a coveted spot.

Gus enjoyed swimming in the lake, rolling around dripping wet on the beach sand, and catching rays on a beautiful summer day. His favorite activity hands down, though, was lounging around. Frankly, he really preferred being a "couch potato." Gus was the shortest and slowest dog of the group and with his physical attributes working against him, often missed opportunities to get a good resting place on higher ground. My husband lovingly called him a "low rider."

The rest of the dogs raced each other to the couch or armchairs to claim space when it came time for napping. Time and again, Gus didn't get to

FIGURE 0.1
Our family, left to right: Sammi, Scout, Bo, and Gus ("The Professor"). Story and photograph courtesy of Angela Fern.

where he wanted to go fast enough, and it became evident he wasn't going to take it any longer. But how was he going to get the best seat in the house, the armchair that gave him a wide view of the living room and kitchen?

His strategy was brilliant. He figured out that where he was would be where all the other dogs would want to be. So, when he lost the race once again, he ran to the front window and started barking—as if there was something spectacular going on outside. Invariably, our other dogs vacated the couch or armchairs and sprinted over to the window too and looked out, barking at what they thought he saw. Meanwhile, Gus trotted over to his favorite chair and hopped up, unopposed. GPS. Gus' Positioning System. I admired him. I adored him. I laughed so hard I couldn't breathe. There was absolutely nothing going on outside! It was simply a bullshit ploy.

He earned the nickname "The Professor" after years of outsmarting the other dogs that way every time. He died 2 days shy of his 15th birthday in his favorite chair. We still refer to it as the "good chair" in Gus' honor.

The moral of the story? To get what you want in life—you've simply got to find the way! Doggone it, Gus showed us how to get what he wanted in life—and following the recommendations in this book will do the same for you.☺

Angela Fern, MS

Preface

Life is short—often too short. At one of my sisters' funerals (I lost both of my younger sisters in 2015—one to a cardiac arrest following a surgical procedure, the other to glioblastoma, a debilitating brain cancer), I heard a passage in Rabbi Susan Stone's eulogy that stayed with me. "We live less than the time it takes to blink an eye if we measure our lives against eternity" (which she acknowledged was from Chaim Potok's *The Chosen*). It reminded me of a question that I pondered years earlier: "Can one really make a difference during the flicker of their lifetime?" To me, the answer was addressed by the relevant sentiments of others:

> I believe that we are who we choose to be. Nobody is going to come and save you. You've got to save yourself. Nobody is going to give you anything. You've got to go out and fight for it. Nobody knows what you want except you, and nobody will be as sorry as you if you don't get it. So, don't give up on your dreams.
>
> **Anonymous**

> You are never too old to set another goal or dream a new dream.
>
> **C.S. Lewis**

> You cannot have significance in this life if it is all about you. You get your significance, you find your joy in life through service and sacrifice (for others)—it's pure and simple.
>
> **Paul Tudor Jones**

> If you can dream it, you can do it.
>
> **Walt Disney**

> You don't have to see the top of the whole staircase, the desired destination, just take the first step.
>
> **Anonymous**

> What we are building right now, hour by hour, day by day, is our own future. Whether we construct it with care or indifference, it is the future we will someday occupy.
>
> **Author, broadcaster Mort Crim**

At this point in my career, I've largely accomplished the personal and professional goals that I set out to achieve. Yet, the "ultimate success" is to truly make a lasting difference in the lives of countless others, long after you're gone. Steve Jobs, Henry Ford, Ray Kroc, and Walt Disney, to name just a few, achieved this notoriety. Did you know that next to food and clothing, attaining personal and professional success is rated at the very top of the "hierarchical order" of human needs? All of us want to be successful and live the life of our dreams. The fact of the matter is: EVERYBODY WANTS TO BE SOMEBODY!

Years ago, I came to the sobering realization that leadership, life's opportunities, career advancement, and professional and financial success don't just happen. I learned that, to a large extent, YOU CREATE THEM by demonstrating certain actions and behaviors on a regular basis. In this unique book, I've meticulously chronicled proven behavioral strategies that, if carefully followed on a daily basis, are guaranteed to achieve these objectives—along with a happy and fulfilling life.

> You are your own fortune cookie.
>
> **Car bumper sticker**

This text was written to uniquely offer the reader a compendium of behavioral skills that can empower "success" in today's challenging work environment, including real-world time-tested principles and strategies, e.g., expect the best, exceed people's expectations, look for the good in people and situations, set goals (in writing), visualize yourself achieving your goals, be ferociously persistent, ask for things you want, constantly strive to improve your vocabulary and communication skills, enter into partnerships or collaborations with others who have skills, abilities, or resources you don't have, develop excellent people skills, work hard, and focus on your most productive activities (the 80/20 rule), also known as the Pareto principle. Just like your car's or phone's GPS, these behavior skills, strategies, and secrets can get you from where you are to where you want to go (in life).

In addition, critically important and complementary knowledge, skills, and abilities, including job interviewing, must-know people skills, writing, and public speaking, are covered. In this book, we've scoured the world's literature on these topics, interviewed countless highly successful people, and more to provide one-stop shopping regarding the most proven and practical recommendations for future career success. We've also peppered the text with personal experiences and motivational/inspirational success stories, as well as testimonials/sage advice/quotes from many of the world's most successful people—past and present. To maximize the user-friendly, easily accessible resource information contained in this handbook, lengthy text descriptions have been minimized and replaced by focused section subtitles, complementary tables, boxed highlighted information, self-assessment tests, and figures to reinforce key or salient points, as well as a compilation of memorable success quotes (Appendix A).

Unfortunately, as you'll see, these invaluable life strategies and behavior skills have seldom made it to the educational curriculum of most high schools and universities. In a nutshell, my goal was to develop a book "with legs," that is, one that keeps on giving and includes timeless information for generations to come, involving people in all walks of life, with specific reference to recent high school and college graduates and those in the early stages of their professional careers.

Trust me, there is *magic* within these pages, and in sharing what I've learned with others, I sincerely believe that the messages contained herein, if thoroughly embraced and regularly followed, will have a profound and favorable impact on furthering *your career* and accomplishments—long after the flicker of my lifetime. If I'm right, I'd venture to say that the financial dividends alone will be literally thousands of times what you paid for this book. And that's only a fraction of the benefits you'll receive. Time will tell—and you'll be the judge.

Acknowledgments

With the deepest gratitude, I wish to thank every person who inspired, motivated, and enlightened me through their presence, persona, and publications on how to lead my life——priceless lessons I learned that I've attempted to share in this book.

Many people contribute to the making of a book, and at the risk of leaving some people out, I'd like to publicly thank those mentioned here.

The empowerers begin with my wife Linda for her love, patience, understanding, encouragement, and support. She has helped, in so many ways, to turn countless setbacks over the years into camouflaged opportunities and ultimate successes.

This book, an experiential compendium to achieve real-world career success, and the forerunners of it, gratitude and happiness, would simply not have materialized without the dedication and extraordinary talents of Brenda White. She orchestrated the preparation of this manuscript, serial revisions, and editing of the chapters with patience, endurance, and a unique sense of responsibility. Special thanks are also extended to a graphic artist par excellence, Sue Tomaszycki, for the enormous help she provided with complementary figures and related artwork.

Words cannot express the "once-in-a-lifetime" opportunity that Drs. Seymour Gordon and Gerald C. Timmis provided in hiring me to direct the preventive cardiology/cardiac rehabilitation program at Beaumont Hospital in 1985. Dr. Timmis taught me invaluable lessons that took my writing to greater heights than I ever imagined. Also, sincerest thanks to Beaumont Health, who invariably supported my career aspirations and paid me (with benefits) to do what I loved doing over the past 37 years!

Appreciation and gratitude to Mark Sanborn, an internationally known best-selling author, motivational speaker, and leadership guru, for his generous comments in writing my Foreword.

Heartfelt thanks to Michael Josephson, former law professor and attorney who founded the nonprofit Joseph and Edna Josephson Institute of Ethics. Not only did his pioneering career have a profound and favorable impact on mine, but also, he gave me permission to use his classic poem "What Will Matter" in my final chapter.

I'm indebted to Angela Fern, a dear friend and esteemed colleague, for writing "A Favorite Story," which opens the book, about her beloved yellow Labrador Retriever Gus (aka "The Professor"), who ingeniously showed us how to get what you want in life.

Kudos for their generosity in sharing, without permission or charge, their copyrighted "Satisfaction with Life Scale," by Ed Diener, Robert A. Emmons, Randy J. Larsen, and Sharon Griffin.

Others who influenced the evolution of this book include: Susan Bolotin, publisher and editorial director, Workman Publishing; Linda Konner, literary agent; Randy Brehm, senior editor at Taylor & Francis Group; Marjory Abrams, former executive editor and chief content officer, Bottom Line Inc.; and James Peterson, PhD, owner, Coaches Choice, Healthy Learning, who helped me revamp my Table of Contents.

So many friends, esteemed colleagues, and staff in the American College of Sports Medicine, American Association of Cardiovascular and Pulmonary Rehabilitation, the American Heart Association, and the American Society for Preventive Cardiology have inspired, instructed, and encouraged me over the passing years. Being a member and a fellow of these fine organizations added tremendously to my personal life as well as my professional career. There are far too many colleagues to mention by name who "opened unimagined doors" for me, but you know who you are.

To treasured friends for their unwavering support and enthusiasm for my primary objective in writing this book, that is, "helping young people help themselves." These include: Dr. Gerald C. Timmis; Dr. David and Carla Forst; Dr. William C. Roberts; Professor Weimo Zhu; Dr. Ronald and Barbara Stewart; Kathy Berra; Joseph C. Piscatella; and Dick and Norma Sarns.

Finally, to the esteemed colleagues who provided the praise/endorsements featured on the inside jacket. And, the superb team at Productivity Press I count as friends. Thanks to Michael Sinocchi for believing in *GPS for Success*, to Samantha Dalton for her editorial assistance in bringing the book to fruition, to Kari Budyk, my Project Editor, who adeptly handled content management of this book, and to Nancy J Prabakar, Project Manager at Deanta Global, who oversaw the production of my book, on behalf of Taylor & Francis.

It should be apparent, but if I'm asked to objectively rate my life gratitude, it's captured on the meter here:

GRATITUDE METER

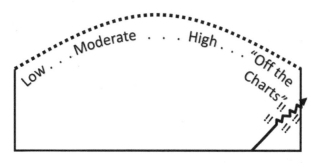

FIGURE 0.2
Gratitude meter.

About the Author

 **Barry A. Franklin, PhD**, is Director of Preventive Cardiology and Cardiac Rehabilitation at Beaumont Health, Royal Oak, Michigan, USA, and Professor of Internal Medicine, Oakland University William Beaumont School of Medicine, Rochester, Michigan, USA. His clinical research interests include the primary and secondary prevention of heart disease; cardiovascular risk reduction; obesity and metabolism; exercise testing/prescription; and lifestyle medicine.

In his early 30s, Franklin intuitively embraced business management/productivity guru Peter Drucker's recommendation that "everyone should find at least one interest outside his/her primary area, and make that secondary pursuit into more than just a hobby." For him, that secondary pursuit, the study of highly successful people in all walks of life, became a passion. Years later, he took what he had learned and developed a college course titled "GPS for Success," which he taught at Central Michigan University (2012–2017). It became one of the most popular courses on campus. Since the mid-1990s, he's participated in countless media (e.g., YouTube TV) and invited presentations on this topic as well as giving themed commencement addresses at major universities.

Dr. Franklin's professional accomplishments have been recognized through a number of honors and awards. He has served as President of the American Association of Cardiovascular Pulmonary Rehabilitation and President of the American College of Sports Medicine as well as Chair, American Heart Association Council on Nutrition, Physical Activity, and Metabolism. In 2010 he was appointed to the national American Heart Association Board of Directors as well as a member of the Administrative Cabinet. Franklin is a past editor-in-chief of the *Journal of Cardiopulmonary Rehabilitation* and prevention and currently holds editorial positions with 15 other scientific and clinical journals.

Dr. Franklin has written or edited more than 700 publications, including 547 papers, 103 book chapters, and 27 books, including this one (*GPS for Success*). He has also narrated 42 educational videos. In 2015, he was named by Thomson Reuters among the *World's Most Influential Scientific Minds* (Clinical Medicine). He has given over 1,000 invited presentations to state, national and international, medical, and lay audiences.

This self-help book captures all he's learned over the past four decades regarding the principles that are the gateway to professional success, with specific reference to sales, business, leadership, and academics. It provides a treasure-trove of proven behaviors that can be learned and refined, gleaned from many of the world's most successful people. Please visit www.drbarryfranklin.com for more on Dr. Franklin, including his complimentary video presentation on the essence of *GPS for Success*.

Section I

A Roadmap for Success

1

My Journey: Inquisitive, Driven, and Goal-Oriented

As a gymnast at Kent State University, my goals as an undergraduate student were largely two-fold: improving my athletic performance and competitive scores on the still rings, and which attractive co-ed I'd be taking out over the weekend. As I approached my senior year, however, I came to the sobering realization that continuing my education mattered and that my current aspirations weren't going to pay the bills or, for that matter, lead to a meaningful and fulfilling professional career, as well as financial security.

Nearly four decades ago, I became fascinated with a simple question: "Why do some people and organizations thrive while others seem to tread water and merely survive?" After 10 years of undergraduate and graduate education, ultimately culminating in a PhD (Physiology) from The Pennsylvania State University, it seemed somewhat paradoxical to me that virtually no college course had prepared me for the real-life career challenges and professional and interpersonal skills I'd need to thrive in the healthcare environment that I was now in. To find out, I began reading everything I could on leadership and success strategies, and carefully studied the "stars" in their respective fields. I devoured books by Napoleon Hill, Claude Bristol, Earl Nightingale, Zig Ziglar, Tony Robbins, Jim Collins, Steven Covey, Jack Canfield, and Rhonda Byrne, to name just a few. Moreover, I interviewed many highly successful people, including my good friend and esteemed colleague, Joseph C. Piscatella, a "million selling" book author; Lloyd Reuss, former president of General Motors; and Sam Fox, a highly successful entrepreneur, who served as the former ambassador to Belgium—as well as many others. Then, I put on my

DOI: 10.4324/9781003260387-2

scientific, research-based hat and carefully reviewed the few studies that systematically addressed the characteristics of highly successful people. Were there common behaviors they exhibited? You bet there were!

In my early 30s, I intuitively embraced Peter Drucker's recommendation that "everyone should find at least one interest outside his/her primary area and make that secondary pursuit more than just a hobby." For me, that secondary pursuit, the study of highly successful people in all walks of life, became a passion. In essence, I followed Malcolm Gladwell's advice and have now devoted far more than 10,000 hours to studying the characteristics of highly successful people using the methodologies of a research scientist (my academic training). I simultaneously conducted a sobering experiment on myself. When I started applying these behavioral skills and strategies to my own life, I began attracting good luck and related professional opportunities, but in an exponential manner. I married the perfect spouse (Linda; now 51 years ago) for the journey ahead, landed a dream job at one of the preeminent academic, teaching, and research medical centers in the United States, William Beaumont Hospital, Royal Oak, MI, and traveled the world, generally lecturing on someone else's nickel. I published more than 700 papers ... authored, co-authored, or edited 27 books ... served as president of two national professional associations as well as the editor-in-chief of two scientific/clinical journals ... and in 2015, was named by Thomson Reuters among the World's Most Influential Scientific Minds (in the Clinical Medicine category)—rare for a PhD!

I tell my students and junior colleagues, "Don't discount this gray-haired professor as a bona fide life/career coach! If you take the time to hear me out, it will be well worth your while." As the late professor Randy Pausch, author of *The Last Lecture*, emphasized to his devoted students, *"experience is often the most valuable thing you have to offer."*

Impetus for this book? Contemporary surveys have consistently shown that modern-day college graduates don't feel well equipped to face the real world. According to the American Council on Education, institutions of higher learning and their faculties have a critical role in developing high-quality relevant curricula that equip students with *broad life and career skills* that empower them to contribute meaningfully to their communities and the workplace. These underappreciated "soft skills" include: the power of positive associations and collaboration; essential people skills; interviewing; problem solving; goal setting; cultivating motivation, focus, and commitment; the boomerang effect of serving others; dealing with setbacks; the virtues of patience and persistence; the potency of preparedness; writing and speaking expertise; understanding the laws of attraction and sow and reap; the invaluable dividends of organizational/ association membership; and the #1 success strategy—taking action.

To address these topics and more, based on my longstanding interest in studying highly successful people in all walks of life, I developed a course at Central Michigan University entitled "GPS for Success," which I taught from 2012 to 2017—a course that received rave reviews and was consistently ranked #1 by the students who enrolled in it (see box, *Student Praise for GPS for Success*). After reading their overwhelmingly positive feedback and complimentary comments on the course, I realized that we were filling a critical void in their educational curriculum, and that I was on to something BIG. When I stopped teaching the course 3 years ago, I started writing the textbook for future generations and titled it *GPS for Success: Skills, Strategies, and Secrets of Superachievers*. In it, I've captured the essence of all I've learned over the past four decades regarding the life skills and strategies that are the gateway to success. Although this is the 27th book I've authored, co-authored, or edited, it's by far the best of the rest—likely my "Last Lecture." Why? Because it includes *life-changing advice*!

STUDENT PRAISE FOR GPS FOR SUCCESS*

I still have the notes I took from the lectures and a few of your inspirational quotes have stuck with me throughout the years and one being: "The secret to success is to give people more than they expect." Your strategies and advice helped me "turn the faucet on." And this e-mail is to thank you for your extraordinary advice and simply for your inspiration. Like Thomas J. Watson said, "The way to succeed is

---

* Over the years, students taking the course were requested to provide feedback to the Department Administration, either with their designated signature or anonymously. Unfortunately, this course had no complementary textbook. *GPS for Success* was written to fill this void for high school graduates and college/university students around the country, and to provide a needed resource that specifically targets young adults and early career professionals (e.g., 18–35 years of age). Others, however, would undoubtedly benefit from the comprehensive success principles described in this handbook.

to double your failure rate." He was right. Take care and God Bless
....

A.P.

I think this class has taught me more than any other class I've ever taken at Central Michigan University. I wish everyone "seized the opportunity" to take it. It was worth way more than the cost of a one credit hour course.

Anonymous

What I learned this past weekend will stick with me for the rest of my life and has reminded me to keep going after all of my dreams.

L.M.

Out of the 100⁺ credits I have accumulated in my undergraduate career, I feel this single credit will turn out to be the most beneficial and influential of them all.

M.M.

You have truly inspired me to go the extra mile for what I believe in and a lifelong goal of helping others. Continue to change the lives of young professionals and students. You exceeded my expectations for this class and I guarantee that I will remember you and this course for a lifetime. I now feel I have the duty to be an honest, hard-working, caring professional in your honor. Thank you!

J.A.

You get strategies on success that you don't get in "normal" college courses, and things you **desperately** need to know.

S.C.

Very valuable life lessons not taught in regular college courses or any level courses. Well worth the cost of a one credit hour undergraduate course at Central Michigan University. I have a business major brother coming to CMU next year that would HIGHLY benefit from this information.

Anonymous

Practical skills that I will carry with me throughout the rest of my career and life. Excellent course. I feel that everything covered will tremendously help me as I develop into my career and professional life.

K.K.

I really think this course is useful because it applies to real life. I've never had a course that made me feel as empowered and invested in my future as this one has. I really mean that. My only criticism is how short the course was—I wish it would have been even longer, so that we could have obtained ever more information.

Anonymous

Real-life, applicable information. Current/relevant to students pursuing a career in any field. Worth more than the cost of a one credit hour undergraduate course.

Anonymous

This course taught me so many things, I'm beyond happy I took it. Very helpful for future endeavors in any career field. I truly enjoyed it and will highly recommend it to others.

Anonymous

I've learned more in this day and a half course about the "real world" than I have in the past 4 years of undergraduate school. This course offered practical and inspiring information.

Anonymous

I thought this course was amazing and it really made me think about what I need to change in my life to become successful. I loved hearing all the success stories—it made it more relatable to my life.

Anonymous

What captivated me was how relatable your remarks were to me personally. In the midst of all the chaos of an ending semester, I could not have heard your "strategies for success" at a more perfect time. Because of you, I have regained my self-confidence. You have revitalized the notion of, "If it is to be, it is up to me." I believe in myself now more than ever. You have also shifted my perspective on what truly matters, that is, helping others around me to achieve as well. I make you this promise: I will rehearse and practice your strategies every day to the best of my ability to become a highly successful person. I hope you continue to inspire other students the way you inspired me.

M.T.M.

CARPE DIEM

When I lecture on *success*, I often start by playing a brief clip from the film *Dead Poets Society* starring the late Robin Williams as school teacher John Keating. I can't hit "play" for you readers, but here's a link to see the video—it's only 3 minutes, and well worth the watch: https://www.youtube .com/watch?v=veYR3ZC9wMQ. Below is a transcription of an excerpt from that clip. To set the scene: It's the first day of class at this all-male boarding school in the 1950s. Mr. Keating enters whistling Tchaikovsky's 1812 Overture, invites the class to follow him out into the hallway, and asks a student to read the first stanza of the poem "To the Virgins to Make Much of Time" by Robert Herrick:

Student 1:	"Gather ye rosebuds while ye may. Old Time is still a-flying. And this same flower that smiles today, tomorrow will be dying."
Mr. Keating:	Thank you, Mr. Pitts. "Gather ye rosebuds while ye may." The Latin term for that sentiment is "Carpe diem." Now who knows what that means?
Student 2:	Carpe diem. That's "Seize the day."
Mr. Keating:	Very good, Mr. … Meeks. Another unusual name. Seize the day. "Gather ye rosebuds while ye may." Why does the writer use these lines?
Student 3:	Because he's in a hurry.
Mr. Keating:	No! Ding!! Thank you for playing anyway. Because we are food for worms, lads. Because, believe it or not, each and every one of us in this room is one day going to stop breathing, turn cold, and die. I would like you to step forward over here and peruse some of the faces from the past. *[Close-up on old class photos displayed in the glass encasements.]* You've walked past them many times. I don't think you've really looked at them. They're not that different from you, are they? Same haircuts. Full of hormones, just like you. Invincible, just like you feel. The world is their oyster. They believe they're destined for great things, just like many of you. Their eyes are full of hope, just like you. Did they wait until it was too late to make from their

lives even one iota of what they were capable? Because, you see, gentlemen, these boys are now fertilizing daffodils. But if you listen real close, you can hear them whisper their legacy to you. Go on, lean in. Listen. Do you hear it?

(whispering) Carpe.

Hear it?

(whispering) Carpe ... Carpe diem ... Seize the day, boys ... Make your lives extraordinary.

That film clip had a profound impact on me when I first saw it in 1989. It made me ponder the question—what is an extraordinary life? Is it happiness, being well educated, achieving financial security, helping others, making a difference, contributing to the betterment of our society, experiencing the "flavor" of other cultures (worldwide), feeling passionate about what you do, achieving preeminence in the field that you select, or perhaps "sowing the seeds" for all these objectives via a successful personal life and professional career?

I came to realize the unflagging power of the adage, "as you sow, so shall you reap, all the years of your life." And, what constitutes "*success*"? Without question, there are many different interpretations, based on personal goals, aspirations, and desires. Is "success" synonymous with being rich, famous, or happy? Certainly, it is possible to be rich, famous, or both, yet not happy, or be neither rich nor famous, but happy. It's largely your mindset or perspective, at any given time in your life. For many, success means $UCCE$$—professional notoriety, pioneering entrepreneurship, savvy investing, any approach to financial wealth. The best definition of success I've ever read goes like this: "Success is the progressive realization of a worthy goal," or in some cases, "... the pursuit of a worthy ideal." It means that anyone who's on course toward the achievement of a worthwhile goal for them (and society) is currently successful.

And now I offer that same challenge to you—seize the day. How will you make your life extraordinary? My "GPS for Success" and related skills, strategies, and secrets of superachievers can, without question, help you attain your life goals.

How do you make yourself stand out from the crowd? Are there particular personality characteristics or traits that people have who are really happy and successful in their personal life, their work, or ideally both? Are there things they do on a day-to-day basis, whether consciously or unconsciously? Here's what I've learned, from personal experiences, all of the books I've read, and all of the people I've interviewed, are the keys to being personally and professionally successful. They're housed in the remaining chapters: foundations for your journey (Chapter 2); 10 steps for success (Chapters 3–12), additional strategies and tactics for success (Chapters 13 and 14); Appendix A, memorable quotes on success; and, Appendix B, additional success resources.

Let's start with your journey.

2

Your Journey: Love, Luck, Responsibility, and Serving Others

LOVE **WHAT YOU DO**

One of the common characteristics of highly successful people that I found in my research was articulated by the late Steve Jobs: "The only way to do great work is to love what you do. If you haven't found it yet, keep looking." His advice got my attention. Pretty bright guy. So, when young people say to me, "Well, I'm not sure what I want to do," I say, "Find out. Do an internship. Go here, go there. Discover what you enjoy, excel at, and really turns you on. That will get you on the road to success."

These sentiments were echoed by Pat Williams, who, at the time, was senior vice president of the Orlando Magic basketball team: "Figure out what you love to do as young as you can, and organize your life around figuring out how to make a living at it." *Essentially, get somebody to pay you to do what you love to do for the rest of your life.* For me, I learned early on what I loved to do, and was pretty good at. Working at a major medical center, helping patients prevent chronic disease and helping others who had experienced a cardiac event or had undergone heart bypass surgery and/or coronary angioplasty in optimally managing their cardiovascular disease. My responsibilities involved directing the cardiac rehabilitation program, diagnostic and functional cardiovascular testing, drafting policies and procedures, staff hiring and training, embracing safety and quality assurance standards, personnel issues, counseling patients, formulating exercise prescriptions, serving on committees, mentoring medical students, residents, cardiology fellows, and staff, media interviews, clinically relevant volunteer association involvement, presentations, as

DOI: 10.4324/9781003260387-3

well as teaching, writing, and research. And, I got Beaumont Health to pay me to do that over the last 37 years.

Simultaneously, I intuitively embraced two of Peter Drucker's (the father of modern management) "success pearls" early in my career. I identified and cultivated a keen interest outside my primary area (preventive cardiology/cardiac rehabilitation), that is, the study of highly successful people in all walks of life. Drucker also emphasized the importance of leaving something behind when you are gone. Similarly, the late Steve Jobs said: "You've got to put something back into the flow of history that's going to help your community, help other people ... so that 20, 30, 40 years from now ... people will say, this person didn't just have a passion; he cared about making something that other people could benefit from." Beyond family/ friends, the patients I counseled, and the staff/students I mentored are my enduring scientific and research publications. My expectation, however, is that this particular book, *GPS for Success*, will truly be my lasting legacy, benefitting countless people worldwide and future generations.

MAKE YOUR OWN *LUCK*

How to Make Luck is a book I read years ago by Marc Myers. It highlights an important underlying temporal relation that highly successful people have come to realize: In many respects, "luck occurs when opportunity meets preparation." Accordingly, prepare yourself for future opportunities that *will* arise. Myers suggests that "up to 95 percent of all the lucky (or unlucky) things that happen to you, happen because of things you did, or you didn't do." They're not coincidences. *To a large extent, you make your own destiny.*

Several years ago, we were hiring an additional nurse for our cardiac rehabilitation department. Through a series of interviews, we narrowed down 10 candidates to the final 2—but it remained a toss-up. I said to our manager, "Let's think about this a bit more before we decide who we are going to select." That weekend, I got a thank you card from one of the nurses, which included a handwritten note that read, "Dear Dr. Franklin, Thanks for your time and your consideration. I really enjoyed meeting everyone and I would love to be part of the Beaumont team. If I'm fortunate enough to be selected—you won't be disappointed." When I came in on Monday and mentioned the card to our manager, he said, "I received a thank you card in the mail, too." We looked at each other and simultaneously agreed: We now knew which nurse we were going to select. That's not luck! She went a little bit further than every other nurse by sending a handwritten card thanking us—reinforcing her continued interest in the position. To a large extent, people make their own luck. You've simply got to be willing to do a bit more than your peers, counterparts, and competitors.

TAKE *RESPONSIBILITY* FOR YOUR LIFE

What else did I learn? Highly successful people take 100 percent responsibility for their life. After a talk I gave years ago at Kent State University about self-responsibility, a student came up to me and asked, "Dr. Franklin, do you know of the 10 most powerful two-letter words?" (see Figure 2.1) I admitted I did not. "Well, here they are," she replied. I subsequently learned that her quote was attributed to an American painter, William H. Johnsen.

People who take 100 percent responsibility for their life are invariably the most successful.

A MEMORABLE COMPANY FUNERAL AND MOMENT OF SELF-REFLECTION

One morning, company employees arrived at work to find a sign on the door. It read: "The person who has been hindering your growth in this company has passed away. Please come to the funeral in the large meeting room." Puzzled, people began filing in to pay their last respects, everyone wondering, "Who was this?" One by one, they looked into the coffin and saw—a mirror, reflecting their faces as they peered inside. A sign next to the mirror said: "There is only one person who is capable of setting limits to your growth. It is YOU."

You're the only person who can ignite your career pathway, the only person who can influence your happiness, your aspirations, and your success. Your life does not change when circumstances change. It changes when YOU change, when you go beyond the beliefs and

The 10 Most Powerful Two-Letter Words

If It Is To Be, It Is Up To Me.

FIGURE 2.1

habits that limit you, and when you accept the fact that you are 100 percent responsible for your life.

FOCUS ON *SERVING OTHERS*: THE REWARDS WILL COME

Albert Einstein, one of the 20th century's universally acknowledged geniuses, was once asked, "Doctor, why are we here?" Einstein turned to his questioner in surprise and replied, "We are here to serve other people." It's so simple. When I first thought about his response, and considered all the people I've interviewed or studied over the years, the one common denominator in everyone who was highly successful, who clearly enjoyed life, and who could be described as happy or content was that they admirably served others. No surprise—Einstein was right. He had it right! Focus on your contributions, on serving others, and the rewards will come.

CULTIVATE INTEREST IN OTHERS—AND HELPING THEM!

Tolstoy knew what he was talking about when he said, "We love people not for what they can do for us, but for what we can do for them." It's the fundamental ingredient in the recipe for success in life. When you become genuinely interested in others and helping them get what they want, you'll automatically become successful. The more people you help, and the more you do for them, the greater the rewards (for you).

Similarly, Rick Warren, author of *The Purpose-Driven Life*, said that the only way to get more of what really matters in life is to put more into it. He went on to say that each of us was created for a reason, and that acquiring worldly goods is not the reason. *The true measure of success is not how many people serve us, but how many people we serve.* Although attaining a purpose-driven life is rewarding, it is not always easy. Why? Because it often involves putting the needs of others ahead of our own needs. Nevertheless, the ultimate rewards can be enormous—for those who provide meaningful products, services, or contributions to the needs and well-being of countless others.

Several years ago, while I was serving as a visiting professor in Thailand, we had the opportunity to stay one night in the home of one of the country's wealthiest and most successful couples, who were out of the country. These people, when learning about our upcoming visit, were particularly generous in offering their home, food, house staff, and grounds, situated on a beautiful winding river, to my wife and me, and to the contingent of professors and students who were serving as our hosts and guides. But the take home message I'll always remember was walking upstairs with my wife to our magnificent wood-paneled bedroom. On the wall, adjacent to the stairwell, we found a huge sign, in English, that read: *"We become successful by helping other people to become successful."* Wow, I thought. I've just traveled halfway around the world to receive the universal secret to success! It also reinforced something else I learned about the superachievers on our planet. Most of the rich, famous, and super successful people that I've met, or studied, GIVE BACK—BIG TIME. More about this later in the book.

Everyone has a "what matters to me" scale with contributions on one side and rewards on the other (see Figure 2.2). In my experience, too many young people, early in their career, focus on the material rewards— the trips, magnificent home, luxury car, clothes, big money, etc. Their attention is on the wrong end of the scale! *Superachievers focus on their*

Our Rewards Equal Our Contributions (You Get What You Give)

FIGURE 2.2

contributions—serving others or helping others fill a void or special need, by inventing products and providing services that entertain or enrich people or help them do things better, or faster, or more efficiently. Their goal is helping you achieve your goal(s). Thoroughly explore all the opportunities right where you are before looking for that elusive pot of gold and never staying at one place long enough to find it (see "Acres of Diamonds" story later in the book). If you do, the rewards will come. In my experience, the people who move up in any organization, that is, those who are regularly promoted, are the ones who focus on their contributions, routinely do more than they are being paid to do, and invariably "raise their hand" when volunteers are requested.

Perhaps the late Zig Ziglar (motivational speaker and success guru) said it best: "You can get anything you want in life if you help enough other people get what they want." *Be an innovator. Identify needed services, leisure-time amusements, or products for the masses and fill the void.* Athletes, entertainers, media personalities (e.g., the late Johnny Carson), and even writers can help fill these essentials of life. Consider what Henry Ford, the Wright brothers, Ray Kroc, Walt Disney, Jeff Bezos, Steve Jobs, and other recent superachievers did with their pioneering visions, serving boundless numbers of people along the way and substantively changing the world we live in.

- Henry Ford introduced the Model T automobile, which revolutionized transportation and American industry via mass production of an affordable car, while simultaneously providing good wages for the people who worked for him. He was obsessed with mechanics and machines, which fueled his passion for mechanical engineering. When this was coupled with his unique and complementary people, management, and efficiency skills, he changed the way people worked, in a synergistic manner, and how they routinely traveled from one place to another. The genius of the man was captivated by some of his most famous quotes; my favorites are shown in the table at the conclusion of this chapter.
- Wilbur and Orville Wright made four short flights at Kitty Hawk, North Carolina, with their first powered aircraft on December 17, 1903. The societal impact this had over time, with evolution and refinement including the commercial, business, and broad cultural implications of flight, and the artistic expression it inspired, changed the world.
- Ray Kroc rose from humble beginnings, including a brief stint selling paper cups, to become one of *Time*'s "Most Important People of the Century," building McDonald's into the most famous fast-food restaurant in America and now, worldwide. He literally changed eating out by providing tasty and relatively inexpensive food with minimal wait times. An innovator, with a penchant for efficiency, Kroc standardized McDonald's franchise operations, including portion sizes, taste, food preparation, packaging, and ingredients. He continued to live by his motto—*providing customers what they wanted.*☺
- Walt Disney was a brilliant animator who created the cartoon character Mickey Mouse—the first to synchronize video and sound. He revolutionized the animation industry and was the founder of futuristic and feel-good theme parks, parks that were safe, clean, and fun, where all of his animations magically came to life. These included Disneyland and Walt Disney World—with versions of these theme parks now throughout the world. An innovator and a dreamer, he was

also an exceptional leader, motivating and empowering those who worked for him to cultivate a collective creative genius. Perhaps one of his most famous quotes was: "If you can dream it, you can do it."

- Jeff Bezos created the multi-national technology company Amazon, which represents a titan of e-commerce, and the go-to site for online shoppers and merchants alike, a modern-day *necessity* for millions of subscribers in the United States. When Amazon launched in 1995, its mission statement was "to be Earth's most customer-centric company, where customers can find and discover anything they might want to buy online, and endeavors to offer its customers the lowest possible prices." This goal continues today, but Amazon customers are worldwide.

- Steve Jobs, in a life spanning just 56 years, co-founded Apple, became a legendary business leader, secured more than 450 patents, and was among the giants of the personal computer revolution. He was also behind the highly successful animation studio Pixar, laid the foundation for future Apple products, changed the way people listen to music through iPods, and revolutionized the smartphone market with the iPhone.

- Finally, a group of superachievers whose pioneering work, in aggregate, has had a profound and favorable impact on the lives of countless people worldwide. These include: Ugur Sahin, Ozlem Tureci; Barney Graham, Jason McLellan, Kizzmekia Corbett; Dimitris Bertsimas, Najat Khan, Michael Li, Omar Skali Lami, Hamza Tazi Bouardi, and Ali Haddad. Who are these people, you ask? Let me give you a few clues. First, because of their training and extraordinary expertise, including years of related research, these individuals "fast tracked" a journey that had previously taken 10 to 15 years, to less than 1 year. Second, regardless of their particular agent's chemistry, each empowers the body with a supply of memory T-lymphocytes and B-lymphocytes that will fight a potentially deadly somatic invader. Third, the three groups of unsung scientists (and their research/clinical associates) represent three major companies: Pfizer, Moderna, and Johnson & Johnson. Fourth, as of September 17, 2021, nearly 6 billon doses have now been administered globally. Yes, you got it: some of the key scientists whose groundbreaking research led to the development of safe and effective vaccines to fight Covid.

HENRY FORD QUOTES TO EMPOWER
YOU TO ACHIEVE ANYTHING

- "Whether you think you can, or you think you can't—you're right."
- "Anyone who stops learning is old, whether at twenty or eighty. Anyone who keeps learning stays young."
- "Failure is only the opportunity more intelligently to begin again."
- "You can't build a reputation on what you are going to do."
- "The only real mistake is the one from which we learn nothing."
- "Obstacles are those frightful things you see when you take your eyes off your goals."
- "Vision without execution is just hallucination."
- "Chop your own wood and it will warm you twice."
- "Nothing is particularly hard if you divide it into small jobs."
- "Coming together is the beginning. Keeping together is progress. Working together is success."
- "One of the greatest discoveries a person makes, one of their great surprises, is to find they can do what they were afraid they couldn't do."
- "The whole secret of a successful life is to find out what is one's destiny to do, and then do it."
- "There is no person living who isn't capable of doing more than he/she thinks he can do."
- "If there is any one secret of success, it lies in the ability to get the other person's point of view and see things from that person's angle as well as your own."

Section II

Steps for Success

3

Be an Optimist: Look for the "Good" in People and Situations

Here's a story to illustrate dueling perceptions: An American shoe company sent two salesmen to the Australian Outback. They wanted to find out whether there was any market for shoes among the Aborigines. They received telegrams from both salesmen. The first said, "No business here. The natives don't wear shoes. I'm coming home." But the second telegram proclaimed, "Great opportunity here. The natives don't wear shoes. If I can convince them of the advantages in wearing shoes, we will have a brand new territory here!" Every day, I see examples of this scenario. Two different people are confronted by the exact same scenario, and one has a positive response to it—and to the other, it is a disaster!

Navigating the "Ups" and "Downs" of Life. Instead of feeling that bad news or negative events that occur in your life are invariably the end of the world, recognize that the most highly successful, positive people view these temporary setbacks as opportunities in disguise. Indeed, W. Clement Stone, a self-made millionaire who mentored countless others in the fundamental principles of success, believed that every person he met or circumstance he encountered was meant to better or enrich him. Essentially, he looked for the "opportunity" in everything and everyone that life threw at him. Similarly, Rick Warren, author of *The Purpose-Driven Life*, emphasized that we need to change the way we think when we encounter a daunting problem. Rather than ask, "Why me?" why not ask, "What can I learn from this challenging experience?"

Consider the person who loses his/her job due to a company downsizing. Two responses are possible. One person might embrace the common "woe is me" mentality, immersing himself in self-doubt, low self-esteem, and

DOI: 10.4324/9781003260387-5

a downward spiral. Unfortunately, this response often leads to paralysis and extended unemployment. Essentially, a double whammy! In contrast, another could view the job loss as a blessing in disguise—ultimately yielding a future professional opportunity with higher pay, greater fulfillment, and better benefits. Perhaps Napoleon Hill summed it up best: "Every negative event contains in it the seed (e.g., opportunity) of an equal or greater benefit."

In summary, whenever temporary setbacks occur, I've gotten into the habit of looking for that "seed" and finding the potential upside, rather than dwelling on the perceived downside. I then think about the exciting new opportunity on a daily basis and rigorously pursue it with the expectation of a favorable outcome. By responding to the temporary setback in this manner, which I refer to as FEAR (False Evidence Appearing Real), we can oftentimes transition bad news or negative events to favorable outcomes. Simply stated, look for the lemonade in lemons. The sooner that you can adopt this mentality or approach, the sooner and more often you'll embrace the mindset of W. Clement Stone, that is, life is a series of "Ups" and "Camouflaged Opportunities." When the latter occur, you simply have to find the seed or opportunity that the event provides and transition it to an "Up."

The strange irony that I've found is that these transitional "Ups," that is, following a temporary setback, are oftentimes more meaningful and of far greater benefit to me than are the pedestrian daily goals that I routinely set and achieve. Accordingly, when I encounter a temporary life setback, I invariably now say to myself: "Wow, life-changing good fortune and a breakthrough goal opportunity are heading my way."

HAPPINESS + OPTIMISM = FUTURE SUCCESS

Psychologist Shawn Achor at Harvard found that rather than success leading to happiness, the reverse is true: Happiness leads to success. Similarly, Professor Martin Seligman at the University of Pennsylvania reports that individuals who score high on optimism/happiness scales are among the most successful people in virtually every field. Why? People who believe that good things invariably happen to them exhibit behaviors that make others more receptive to them.

People Responses are Telling. If I were interviewing you for a position at Beaumont Hospital, and you were currently working at Acme Hospital but looking for a job at our major medical center, I'd probably ask you, "How do you like working for Acme?" And, your answer is, "Well, Acme's okay. They don't have this, and they don't have that. Some of their administrators are downright poor. In addition, their employee training programs and benefits, including paid personal and vacation time off, leave something to be desired." I can tell you right now, the interview is over. I don't want you. I've learned the hard way that if you hire negative people like these, the past is prologue to the future. The right answer is:

> Acme has been fabulous for my career, but you're doing some things at Beaumont in health and wellness that are very exciting, that I'd love to be involved in. Working at Beaumont would give me an extraordinary opportunity to grow professionally, learning new skills and having access to state-of-the art equipment and a nationally recognized medical staff. That's why I'm here.

When interviewing, focus on the positives, and avoid discounting or bad mouthing your university or past/current employers (see Chapter 9— Interviewing section).

Whenever I interview somebody, I show them a piece of paper with a phrase that's printed in bold type and ask, "How do you read that?" I'm hoping they answer, "Opportunity is now here." I'm less likely to hire the person who responds, "Opportunity is no where."

OPPORTUNITY

IS NOWHERE

Hidden Opportunities. People look at the same situations or circumstances every day but have different interpretations. Some are negative. Some are positive. I try to hang around the positive people. And I would contend that that is more often the choice of superachievers. Highly successful people are invariably asking, "Okay, how can we benefit from this situation? How do we make this perceived setback ultimately advantageous or positive for our business or our organization?"

For example, I've had numerous experiences over the years learning that a good or great staff member will be leaving the department to pursue other (perceived as superior) opportunities (see section entitled "Looking for Greener Pastures?" [Chapter 13]) or an advanced degree. Among those remaining, some will invariably flock together, proclaiming what I refer to as the "Chicken Little phenomenon"—that is, "the sky is falling" and the department will never be the same (i.e., as good). "With so and so leaving, we'll be going down the toilet," commented one long-term staff member. Another added, "Oh my, the ship is sinking—perhaps there's time to get off the ship while lifeboats are still available?"

If I've learned anything from previous experiences like these, and via several of my skilled administrative mentors, nothing could be further from the truth! These situations, they'd contend, represent tremendous opportunities for a manager or director to improve their department by finding an even better person to take that person's place. Someone who is highly trained, with professional and interpersonal skills and abilities that go beyond the person you are losing, and one who exemplifies organizational wizardry, stellar communication/computer expertise, a passion for what they do, and the ability to work with people (#1). That person is out there—you simply have to find them.

In summary, you can work miracles by having faith in others. Expect the best from people and situations and be grateful for what you have. Being grateful leads us to attract and create more things to be grateful for. Learn to appreciate yourself and your accomplishments. Don't put off being happy, waiting for something great to happen. Accept and appreciate yourself and your life right now. Stop complaining about the negatives (or perceived negatives), and start talking about the positives. In other words, routinely start looking for "the good" in people you meet or work with and situations that you encounter. *Remember that every negative happening in your life contains within it the seed of an equal or greater benefit.* It's up to you to find it. Embrace this mentality—and you'll lay the foundation for future success.

The "opportunity" that Covid-19 presented: I've been interested in writing a book on this particular topic for many years now. In fact, bits and pieces of this book had been written over the past decade. My file cabinets at home were stuffed with note cards, newspaper and magazine articles, and handwritten notes on behavioral skills and inspirational stories of highly successful people in all walks of life. Yet, I never seemed to have the time to complete it?! The spark that drove me to finally complete a first draft of this book may, in itself, be revealing. Without question, one of the behavior skills of highly successful people is that they "look for the good in people and situations." In this case, it was the horrific, worldwide Covid-19 public health crisis that unexpectedly gave me the opportunity to refocus on this unfinished goal.

Since June 2019, I've been working half-time (20 hours per week) after nearly 35 years of full-time employment at William Beaumont Hospital, Royal Oak, Michigan. During this period, I made consistent progress on the book, dedicating time to it on my days off and during weekends. But in mid-March, 2020, the Covid-19 worldwide pandemic hit. Our outpatient, exercise-based cardiac rehabilitation program was temporarily closed, and our Michigan governor, Gretchen Whitmer, mandated a "stay at home" for a minimum of 2 months—particularly meaningful for at-risk older persons like me. The media constantly repeated the message: "Stay home, stay safe." As things turned out, our cardiac rehabilitation program was closed for nearly 3 months, and I was officially "laid off" for 2 months! Initially, I watched the television in horror over the mounting deaths accruing throughout the United States and worldwide, and marveled at our doctors, nurses, allied health professionals, and administrators who were dealing with the influx of gravely ill Covid-19 patients, not to mention the nationwide shortages in protective medical equipment, face masks, and lifesaving ventilators.

What else would I do? I could watch the continued negative television coverage of the health crisis and initially plummeting economy/stock market, become the ultimate couch potato, reading 8–10 hours per day, transition from being mildly overweight to becoming obese by overeating during this highly stressful period, and/or fret about the social isolation and continued home confinement, conference cancellations, closed restaurants, inability to visit my barber, losing my breadwinner status (i.e., no work, no pay), and unsettling disruption of normal life. Or, I could diligently look for concealed or camouflaged opportunities—was there any "good" in this horrible situation? It was up to me to find it—it was my challenge. To yield the greatest results, I decided to embrace Jim Rohn's incredibly powerful principle of taking massive action in the direction of one of my remaining unfulfilled breakthrough goals—this book. No more excuses—I finally had the time to work on it! Some days, 8 to 10⁺ hours.

I wrote on one of my 3 × 5 index notecards that my goals during the Covid-19 crisis would be to stay healthy; respond to all work-related and professional communications in a timely manner; regularly reach out to family, friends, and colleagues; use my treadmill at home, or walk regularly; complement my invigorated exercise commitment (no excuses) by eating even more healthily (a distinct advantage of home cooked meals); and, yes, to finally finish writing a lingering goal for several years now—my *GPS for Success* book. The rest is history! All of these goals were accomplished, and the worldwide devastation of the Covid-19 crisis may soon (hopefully) be in the rearview mirror—thanks to the scientific community's accelerated development of safe and effective coronavirus vaccines.

4

Be Passionate: Believe, Act, Achieve

There is an overwhelming body of evidence in the self-help literature, supported by countless anecdotal reports, that *you become what you think about*. Virtually everything that was ever created or achieved first started as an "idea" in someone's mind. Perhaps Napoleon Hill, author of the classic *Think and Grow Rich*, summed it up best when he said, "What the mind can conceive and believe, it can achieve." Indeed, the beginning of accomplishing your goals and living your dreams resides in initially thinking about what you want and in the power of visualization. *These are widely considered the springboard for goal achievement and ultimate success.*

Successful people visualize their goals and think about them daily. Claude Bristol referred to this repeated repetition on the subconscious mind as the "tap, tap, tap, tap," and the power that it has on changing people's perceptions and behaviors is mindboggling. Good times to do this are before going to sleep or immediately upon awakening. Athletes have used visualization techniques to improve their performance, not only at these times, but also as a preface to and during competition. For example, Tiger Woods envisioned the golf ball in flight and where it would land—immediately before he hit it! Arnold Schwarzenegger spent considerable time, when he wasn't training, visualizing what it would be like to win Mr. Universe. The most powerful computer we have at our disposal is our subconscious mind—but most people don't effectively use it. Just like our car's or phone's global positional system (GPS), it can be programmed to get you to where you want to go. You've simply got to picture the destination, think of it often, and *keep moving* in the direction of your goals.

DOI: 10.4324/9781003260387-6

> **BELIEVING: A HARBINGER OF ACHIEVING**
>
> Harry Lorayne, the world's leading expert on mind and memory training, contends that "believing that you can do something is tantamount to accomplishing it." Accordingly, using subtle and repeated self-suggestion, start setting your sights on higher goals than you ever imagined. Almost all famous athletes and life "superachievers" have embraced visualization and mind modulation, either consciously or unconsciously, as the catalyst for their ultimate success.

THE POWER OF VISUALIZATION AND THE LAW OF ATTRACTION

I've read dozens of self-help books … thousands of pages. Books like Napoleon Hill's *Think and Grow Rich*, Claude Bristol's *TNT: The Power Within You*, *TNT: It Rocks the Earth*, and *The Magic of Believing*, Earl Nightingale's *The Strangest Secret*, Jack Canfield's *The Success Principles*, and the blockbuster best seller, Rhonda Byrne's *The Secret*. And here's the key take home message of all of them: YOU BECOME WHAT YOU THINK ABOUT. Concrete goals, objectives, and desires that come into your mind, especially if you think about them often (e.g., daily), ultimately come to you. It's called the *Law of Attraction*. In essence, thinking about something you want and its regular visualization activates the Law of Attraction—drawing into your life the collaborators, resources, and circumstances you will need to achieve your goal. Specifically, with consistent visualization of a worthy goal or objective, you will be more likely to "take action" to make the dream a reality, and over time, it will be attracted to you. Perhaps Dr. David Schwartz, author of *The Magic of Thinking Big*, summed it up best: "When you believe something's impossible, our mind goes to work to prove why. When you believe, really believe, something can be done, your mind goes to work and helps you find a way to do it." The problem? Most people are thinking about what they don't want and worrying about things they can't control. Then, they wonder why what they don't want shows up over and over again.

The impetus for one of the most popular books ever published? When Jack Canfield and Mark Victor Hansen collaborated on their first *Chicken Soup for the Soul*® book, compiling inspirational, true stories they had heard from audience members over the years, they took a copy of the *New York Times* best-seller list and scanned *Chicken Soup for the Soul*® into the #1 position in the "Paperback Advice, How to and Miscellaneous" category. As a constant reminder of their aspiration, they printed several copies of the poster and hung them up around the office. Less than 2 years later, their book was #1 in that category and stayed there for more than 1 year! To date, it's sold more than 11 million copies around the world, and the entire book series of over 250 titles has now been translated into 43 languages, with more than 500 million copies sold. The take home message? It's hard to dispute that the evolution of the first *Chicken Soup for the Soul*® book was fueled, at least in part, by the Law of Attraction, which was regularly reinforced by the motivational, affirmational, and ingenious posters these authors surrounded themselves with early on.

Listed in the following are real-life examples of the Law of Attraction in amateur athletes, a well-known actor, a doctor of science, a prisoner in the Vietnam War, and a healthcare professional/professor (me).

A SUB 4-MINUTE MILE? THE STORY OF ROGER BANNISTER

In the early 1950s, the general belief was that the 4-minute mile was not medically possible. Despite the naysayers, Roger Bannister thought otherwise. He constantly thought about the sub 4-minute mile, believed he could achieve it, and kept moving toward that goal—shaving off 2 seconds one month, 1 second the next. On May 6, 1954, at Iffley Road Track in Oxford, England, he did the impossible—running the mile in 3 minutes, 59.4 seconds. And in doing so, he clearly changed the attitudes of many. Just 46 days later, John Land of Australia ran the mile even faster: His time was 3 minutes, 57.9 seconds. And then, the dominos really began to fall. In the following year, 1955, 37 runners from around the world broke the established "4 minute barrier," and in 1956, 300 runners broke the record.

Lessons learned? When you abandon your perceived limits, it's amazing what you can accomplish. *Believe, act, and achieve.* But perhaps Bannister captured the essence of his achievement when he stated: "The individual who can drive himself/herself further once the effort gets painful, is the one who will win." This applies not only to road races, but to winning in life. And as the rankings in the professional golf tour will substantiate (see page 173), it pays to be just a little bit better than the next person or, for that matter, your competitors (in life).

THE PHELPS PHENOMENON

I'm a big fan of the Olympic swimmer Michael Phelps. I was in awe of his performance in the 2008 Olympics, when he beat his nearest competitor, the second-place finisher, by one *one-hundredth of a second* in the 100-meter butterfly. I thought, "How the hell can anybody beat a competitor by one one-hundredth of a second?" Then I picked up the newspaper the next day, and it eerily reinforced the Law of Attraction. "So, I think, in my dreams, I always wanted it," Phelps said, when asked by the NBC interviewer if he ever thought he'd pull this off … "And I guess believing all along I could do it goes a long way. The biggest thing I've been thankful for is I've been able to use my imagination. When people said, 'It's impossible, it can't be done,' that's where my imagination came into play." What matters most is how you see yourself. Phelps repeatedly visualized himself winning the race ahead of time, acted with a scientifically based, high-volume, high-intensity, physical training program to achieve that objective, and won it by one one-hundredth of a second.

JIM CARREY'S CLIMB UP THE LADDER: A REMARKABLE COINCIDENCE?

You all know the zany actor-comedian-entertainer, Jim Carrey. Well, here are some things about him you may not know. When he was a child, Carrey's father lost his job, and for a while, the family lived in a camper van on a relative's lawn. Carrey's start, as a stand-up comedian and doing impersonations, bombed badly. A year later, he dropped out of high school to focus on his career. He daydreamed of huge success and imagined himself entertaining the world. At 19 years of age, he headed to Hollywood—but success was elusive.

In 1985, a broke and depressed Carrey drove his old beat-up Toyota up winding Mulholland Drive, where he frequently parked it, overlooking the city of Los Angeles, and daydreamed of success. To soothe his dejection and simultaneously "plant the seed of THINKING BIG," Carrey made an audacious, futuristic decision. He wrote himself a check for $10 million "for acting services rendered," post-dated it 10 years later, and kept it in his wallet. The check remained there over the next decade, as a constant reminder, withering over time.

Call it a remarkable coincidence, but 10 years later, Carrey learned he was cast in the movie *Dumb and Dumber* for—you guessed it—$10 million. However, he made millions more with other blockbuster movies, including *Ace Ventura* and *Pet Detective*! *The take home message? If you're constantly thinking about what you want, you'll attract even more of it (than you ever imagined).*

Although the initial $10 million paycheck might be chalked up to the Law of Attraction, I believe that the catalyst was actually the written check, which remained in Carrey's wallet for 10 years, that did the trick. Whatever happened to the check? When Carrey's father died shortly thereafter, he slipped it into the casket to be buried along with his dad.

A LIFESAVER? THE STORY OF LOUIS PASTEUR

They said, "It could not be done. You can't kill germs that you can't see." But a man, living in France, a doctor of science, believed he could do just that. "I must find the rabies germs that hide inside people and make them sick—so sick that they die. I believe I can," Louis Pasteur would repeatedly say. And because he believed in himself, he kept on working in his laboratory in Paris, knowing that when he did find the invisible enemy—for example, rabies germs—he could help make many sick people well again.

Ultimately, Pasteur would have the opportunity to test his theories—and belief in himself. A young boy, Joey (Joseph) Meister, living in Germany, was bitten 14 times by a rabid dog and, shortly thereafter, became gravely ill. His mother, hoping for a miracle, read in the local newspaper about a doctor of science, living in France, who believed he had found a way to save the lives of people like Joey. Following a hurried (and harried) carriage trip, Joey and his parents arrived at Louis Pasteur's door, where Pasteur welcomed them. "Dr. Pasteur, we've come a long way to see you—our son was bitten by a mad dog, foaming at the mouth, and he's now very sick. Can you help us?" Joey's mother bravely asked. "Perhaps," replied Pasteur. "I have found a method to kill the invisible enemy, the rabies germs that hide inside sick animals, via a vaccine that I've invented." But Pasteur was reluctant to give the rabies vaccine to the boy. Why? Because Joey would be the very first person that the vaccine would be tried on—and no one knew whether it would work or, for that matter, be dangerous to a little boy. Fortunately, two physicians convinced Pasteur to proceed, because the boy would surely die without the vaccine, and Pasteur just might have the remedy. Pasteur did have the lifesaving treatment for Joseph Meister, who recovered and subsequently became a gatekeeper at the Pasteur Institute—for the rest of his life.

Pasteur, initially as a chemist and later as a bacteriologist, continued his pioneering scientific investigations, because he continued believing in himself, and ultimately discovered the cures for silkworm disease and anthrax as well as for rabies. He also invented a process to keep milk from spoiling, a process that is still used today to keep milk free from germs. It's called pasteurization. His "believe I can" attitude regarding the challenges he encountered in life truly enabled him to become a lifesaver for generations to come.

EIGHTEEN HOLES IN HIS MIND: THE POWER OF VISUALIZATION

Score: 94—————7 years————>74

Major James Nesmeth was an average weekend golfer, typically shooting in the mid-to-low 90s. Jim was also a pilot who had a higher calling—flying combat missions over North Vietnam when the war broke out. Sadly, he was shot down, captured as a prisoner of war, and confined to a small cage for the next 7 years. Dealing with social isolation and having only the bare essentials for existence, he knew he had to do something constructive with his mind to occupy his time and combat loneliness and depression.

What did he do? He put his imagination to work for him, visualizing himself playing a round of golf (18 holes) on his favorite course, 7 days a week. He vividly pictured every detail of play, several hours a day, considering club selection, his golf swing, clothes and shoes, weather, birds chirping, warm sun, wind, rain (some days), trees, water hazards, slopes of the course, and sand traps—visualizing every detail and outcome (where the ball landed with each shot)—from tee to green. Essentially, it was James Nesmeth watching a movie of himself, coping with the wind, weather, and an occasional tree obstructing his view to the green—purposefully experiencing the exhilaration of a great shot, and affirming it by stating "great shot," and the despair when his ball landed in a sand trap or in the water.

During his solitary confinement, he became emaciated and deconditioned, experiencing the ravages of muscle atrophy. However, his subconscious mind was challenged daily by the multitude of imaginary situations that one can encounter during a round of golf. After he was released from prison, the first time that he returned to the golf course, he shot a 74—shaving 20 strokes off his previous average. This legendary story about the power of visualization reminded me of the Albert Einstein (winner, Nobel Prize for Physics) quote, years earlier: "Imagination is the preview of life's coming attractions." It's so true!

Achieving success in life involves many of the same mental strategies. Decide career-wise where you want to go and lock it in, just like you would the final destination via your car's GPS. Then use goal setting, affirmation, visualization, and unwavering *action*, perhaps the single most important success skill (see Chapter 6), to guide you moving forward. Affirmations are statements we make to ourselves that reflect our views of who we are and what we want. They can influence our feelings, thoughts, and actions. Challenged by something you've never done? Tell yourself it's easy to do, and repeat it often every day. If you hear something often enough, you'll begin to believe it … the tap, tap, tap, tap of the same message into your subconscious mind. Stay focused, and even if you make a wrong turn, the GPS will recalculate and ultimately lead you to your goal or objective. Almost invariably, I've learned, the system works, if you work the system.

EXAMPLES OF THE LAW OF ATTRACTION IN MY LIFE

In another "real-life" experience, I'm pleased to provide you with chronicled examples of successfully applying the Law of Attraction to my own life, that is, identifying serial goals that I wanted to achieve, writing them down and visualizing them often, and most importantly, taking *action* nearly every day, specific to that goal, until it was achieved. Some of these goals, and the year achieved, are shown in the following table.

GOAL	YEAR ACHIEVED
1. Performing an iron cross on the still rings (gymnastics)	1966
2. Getting into a nationally recognized graduate school (University of Michigan)*	1971
3. Achieving my PhD in physiology (Penn State University)	1976
4. Writing/editing my first book	1984
5. Serving as president of a national professional organization (AACVPR, ACSM)	1987, 1999
6. Serving as the editor-in-chief of a major scientific/clinical journal (JCRP; AJMS)	1990, 2001
7. Working at a major medical center (Case Western Reserve University; William Beaumont Hospital)	1977, 1985
8. Authoring or co-authoring 100 peer-reviewed scientific publications	1991
9. Serving as a commencement speaker at a major university	2000
10. Achieving the academic rank of Professor (Physiology; Internal Medicine)	1994, 2010
11. Teaching a university course on "Success Strategies" (Central Michigan University)	2012–2017
12. Recognized by Thomson Reuter's among the World's Most Influential Scientific Minds (Clinical Medicine)	2015
13. Serving as an invited visiting professor at a major university (Rome, Italy)	2018
14. Achieving the academic prestige/notoriety of an "Endowed Chair"	?
15. Writing a national best-selling book to help others achieve their goals	?

* With a C+ undergraduate grade point average; AACVPR, American Association of Cardiovascular and Pulmonary Rehabilitation; ACSM, American College of Sports Medicine; JCRP, *Journal of Cardiopulmonary Rehabilitation and Prevention*; AJMS, *American Journal of Medicine and Sports*.

In many cases, my goals were achieved in multiples (i.e., attracting more of the things I thought about than I ever imagined). I envisioned myself as president of a national professional organization and ended up being president of two different associations. I thought about serving as editor-in-chief for a major scientific/clinical journal and ultimately served in this role for two different publications. A major goal was to author or co-author 100 peer-reviewed publications; today, the number (including chapters and books) now exceeds 700. Finally, I dreamed of writing, co-authoring, or editing a book that would be useful to others—and this one is my 27th! Perhaps song-writer Chris Daughtry summed it up best in his blockbuster hit "I'm going home," when he said:

> Be careful what you wish for,
> Cause you just might get it all. ☺

USE DAILY VISUALIZATION TO ACCELERATE GOAL ACHIEVEMENT

Visualization accelerates the achievement of any goal by activating your subconscious mind to create the pathway to get what you envision. It involves closing your eyes and creating a detailed, vivid image or picture of a desired goal or objective—and seeing it as if it were already achieved or complete. All of us have this awesome power, but most don't use it or use it effectively. It's not rocket science! For example, if your goal is to run a 10-kilometer (6.2 miles) race, regularly think about your goal and visualize yourself crossing the finish line in the time you desire.

Thinking about something you want and regularly visualizing it activates the subconscious mind and the *Law of Attraction* and heightens internal motivation to TAKE ACTION to achieve your goals and dreams. If done on a daily basis, repeated over time (tap, tap, tap, tap), it essentially transforms you into a magnet, attracting the collaborators, resources, and opportunities needed to get you what you want. Skeptical? Based on the stories I've shared with you in this chapter, and countless others, it's been unequivocally proven to work. And if it's worked for me and others, it can work for you. If you "believe," "act" accordingly, and keep moving in the direction of your dreams, you'll "achieve" (the subtitle of this chapter).

The technique itself, that is, visualization, may represent the 10 most important minutes of your day, ideally 5 minutes before going to sleep and another 5 minutes upon awakening. For many years now, I've used a small 4 × 6 index card to list a number of prioritized goals that I'm working on.

I review each goal for 15–20 seconds, closing my eyes, and envision seeing the goal and experiencing the immense satisfaction of achieving it. I also mentally recite an affirmation or a motivating statement to support my visualization. For example, relative to this book project: "I am writing a book that will be embraced by people worldwide—one that will become a great resource for many in the coming years and, in doing so, will help countless young professionals live the life that they imagine."

When a goal is completed (or accomplished), it's crossed off the list on the index card and ultimately replaced with another future goal. Believe it or not, using visualization and this simple goal setting methodology, more than 90 percent (to date) of my personal and ambitious breakthrough professional goals have been achieved over the years—whether it's performing an iron cross on the still rings, writing or editing a book, serving as president of a national association, traveling the world via invited lectures, or giving the commencement address at a major university. Did I come from a wealthy, influential family, did I attend a prestigious Ivy League undergraduate university, did I get straight A's as a student, did I succeed because I was svelte and drop-dead handsome—none of the above! I'm just an ordinary guy, admittedly goal-oriented and inquisitive, who has *lived the life that he imagined* by following the principles detailed herein.

An encouraging bonus to keep in mind is that when you achieve one goal, perhaps due to the networking that was involved or the heightened visibility that you gained from it, other unanticipated opportunities invariably arise.

REMEMBER: People contacts (networking) and heightened visibility will open up doors for you in life, leading to unimagined prospects and rewards. You can't know too many people or have too much visibility! Accordingly, you'll find that achieving your goals has a domino or synergistic effect, leading to other goals and opportunities that you never anticipated.

5

Be a Goal Setter: Program Your GPS

If you don't know where you are going, you may wind up someplace else.

Yogi Berra

If you can think it, ink it.

Mark Victor Hansen

A classic Volvo advertisement stated, "On the road of life there are passengers and there are drivers." The most successful people in the world are drivers—they know exactly where they are going. Moreover, they write (or digitalize) their goals ... and look at them often. In an excerpt from one of my favorite books on self-improvement, maximizing productivity, and achieving your career goals, called *Mind Hacking*, Sir John Hargrave wrote:

> "Until it's on paper, it's vapor."

Hargrave contends that the obvious-yet-often-underutilized practice of writing down our ideas, thoughts, resolutions, and GOALS is a magical game-changer. *Writing is a gateway for transforming the world of conceiving (ideas) and believing to a world of achieving.* It is the foundation, providing a catalyst for how our thoughts evolve into specific actions that ultimately culminate in achievements and/or sorely needed products or services. In essence, it is the basement for the house that is subsequently built.

Not convinced? In a 2008 study funded by the National Institute of Health, Kaiser Permanente recruited nearly 1,700 people to help them lose

DOI: 10.4324/9781003260387-7

weight by keeping a food diary (a written or digital list of everything they ate). The results were astounding: The more detailed food records people kept, the more weight they lost. In fact, those who kept daily food records lost twice as much weight as those who kept no records! After 6 months, the average weight loss was 13 pounds, and nearly 7 out of 10 patients lost at least 9 pounds. Knowing their food choices would be recorded, rather than eaten and forgotten, proved to be a powerful motivator to make healthier choices. Furthermore, participants began noticing that they were consuming fewer calories, which could only be understood and appreciated after they wrote it down. These findings, from one of the largest and longest-running weight loss trials ever conducted, resulted in keeping a food diary (i.e., food journaling) at weight loss centers around the country.

THE MAGIC OF GOAL SETTING

In 1921, Dr. Lewis Terman of Stanford University led a fascinating study of 1,528 gifted children (i.e., with genius-level intelligence quotients [IQs]) that evaluated the relationship between IQ and achievement. The major findings (I love this): IQ was not the major ingredient for success. The three top predictors of success were perseverance, self-confidence, and, the #1 factor, the tendency to set goals.

THREE PREDICTORS OF SUCCESS

#1 Tendency to set goals
#2 Self-confidence
#3 Perseverance

THE HARVARD BUSINESS SCHOOL
STUDY ON GOAL SETTING

The magic of goal setting, as it affects later outcomes in life, including income, is further illuminated by a study done at Harvard years ago. (I've never found the exact reference, and plenty of people have debunked it, but I still find the purported results extraordinarily illuminating.) In the Harvard Business School study on goal setting, the graduating class was asked a single question about their goals in life: Have you set written goals and created a plan for their attainment? Prior to graduation, the overwhelming majority (84 percent) of Harvard graduates studied had set no goals other than to find a job. Ten years after graduation, they were making an average of x dollars a year. Among those graduates who had set written goals but had no specific plans (13 percent), their average annual income 10 years out was 2x. However, those remaining Harvard graduates (3 percent) who had both written goals and concrete plans, on average, earned 10x the annual income of their collective classmate counterparts. Regardless of whether the Harvard Business study on goal setting is true or not, numerous other studies have shown that goals are more likely to be achieved if they are written out and planned for. The seven steps to setting S.M.A.R.T.E.R. goals, using this acronym, can be helpful in this regard.

THE 7 STEPS TO SETTING S.M.A.R.T.E.R. GOALS

- **Step #1: "S"—Specific.** This means that you don't just say you want to lose weight; you need to say how many pounds you want to lose and keep off (i.e., 10 pounds). Be as specific as possible in detailing your goals *in writing*. Put a number on it; make it exact or measurable.
- **Step #2: "M"—Meaningful.** This means that your goal should be something important to you (i.e., to truly make a lasting difference in your life or the lives of others by helping them to fill a void or special need).
- **Step #3: "A"—Achievable.** This means that you should set short-term goals that you can actually achieve to overcome inertia and build on your momentum. An example—writing a short chapter for a book you plan to complete within the year.
- **Step #4: "R"—Relevant.** This means that your goals should be compatible with your core values, passions, what you truly want out of life, and/or information that will be helpful in enriching the lives of others.

- **Step #5: "T"—Time-Bound**. This means you have to set an exact date when you plan to achieve these focused goals, ideally on a daily, weekly, or monthly basis.
- **Step #6: "E"—Evaluate**. Because goals can easily be ignored, if you visualize and affirm them (verbally) every single day, you'll be more likely to achieve them.
- **Step #7: "R"—Readjust**. Just as the pilots of a plane flying from one destination to another constantly evaluate and readjust the initial flight plan, you should be doing the same for your goals.

THE IVY LEE METHOD FOR PEAK PRODUCTIVITY

In 1918, Charles M. Schwab, one of the richest men in the world, served as president of the Bethlehem Steel Corporation, the *second-largest steel producer* in the United States at the time. To enhance his edge over the competition (a passion of his), Schwab arranged a site visit with a highly respected productivity consultant named Ivy Lee. He hoped Lee could increase the efficiency of his workforce and discover improved and accelerated methods to accomplish even more.

Schwab summoned him to his office and asked Lee to show him the way to get more things done. Lee, a successful businessman and pioneer in the field of public relations, replied that he needed just 15 minutes with each of Schwab's executives. When asked about his fees, Lee answered that there would be no cost to Schwab unless his recommendations worked. "After three months, you can send me a check for whatever you feel my consulting was worth to you," Lee told Schwab.

During his 15-minute consult with each executive, Ivy Lee explained his five-step approach for achieving peak productivity:

1. At the end of each workday, write down the six most important things you need to accomplish tomorrow—no more, no less.
2. Prioritize the items accordingly (#1, most important, #6 of least importance).
3. Focus on the first task until it's finished or nearly completed before moving on to the second.

4. Approach the remaining items in the same manner, moving unfinished items to a new list of six tasks the next day.
5. Repeat the sequence every workday.

According to Schwab and his associates, the improvement in workforce productivity was absolutely astonishing. What made the "Lee approach" so effective? It was simple, it forced workers to truly prioritize a short "to do" list, and it eliminated the question about what workers should be starting on first the next day.

After the 3-month trial, Schwab was so elated with the progress that he called Lee to his office and wrote him a check for $25,000, which by today's standards, approximates $500,000. Not bad compensation for a few hours of work.

What Are Your Top Six "To Dos" For Tomorrow?

1. _____
2. _____
3. _____
4. _____
5. _____
6. _____

A JAR, SOME ROCKS, AND A LESSON ON PRIORITIZING

A college professor stood in front of his class, placed a one-gallon, wide-mouth glass jar on the table in front of him, then dropped two handfuls of big rocks, some nearly the size of a fist, into the jar. They came right to the top of the jar. The professor then asked, "How many of you students think the jar is full?" Somebody yelled, "Yes," but the professor then proceeded to put some gravel in the jar, which worked its way down through the empty spaces. "How many of you think the jar is full now?" he asked again. This time, the class was on to him, so one young man yelled, "probably not." "You're right," replied the professor, as he poured a cup of sand into the jar. When the class agreed that the jar still wasn't full, the professor confirmed it by now pouring a large glass of water into it. What's the point of the demonstration, the professor asked? One female student replied, "The point is that no matter how full your schedule is, you can always cram in some more." And the professor said, "No that's not the point. The point is that if you don't put the big rocks (i.e., most important) in first, you'll never get them in at all." Whether it's a grant proposal, a report you are working on for the boss, an important thank you note, or a book you are writing—whatever! *Take home message: Prioritizing our goals is like dropping rocks into a jar. If we don't fit the big or most important ones in first, we won't get them in at all* (see Figure 5.1).

FIRST THINGS FIRST

Steven Covey, author of many best-selling self-help books, says "First Things First." In fact, he wrote an entire book about it. He advises everyone to make this one change in how you spend your day: *Work on what is most important before you take care of everything else.* Figure out the most important thing for you to be doing right now. Get up early—and as the Nike commercial says, "Just do it!"

Big Rocks:
Scheduling Your Activities

Big
Rocks

Plus
Gravel

Plus
Sand

Plus
Water

FIGURE 5.1

Many years ago, even before the Covey era, I embraced a goal- or objective-oriented mentality, knowing that I wanted to achieve many, and perhaps even a greater number, of the accomplishments that I watched the leaders in my field attain, specifically in the areas of exercise science, sports medicine, and rehabilitation. In particular, I wanted to help many younger colleagues in the field achieve their goals. Why? Because many people had helped me along the way, and I learned that serving or helping others invariably helped me—and magically led to "good karma" heading my way. I also wanted to contribute, in a prolific manner, to the scientific and clinical literature, serve as the editor-in-chief of a scientific journal, become president of a national professional association, travel the world speaking (on someone else's nickel), and write or edit a book—to name just a few.

I adopted the practice "early to bed, early to rise"—very early, in fact, as I sought to rise even before the proverbial rooster to begin work on my most important goals that day. I generally went to bed around 9:45 or 10 pm, set the alarm clock for 4:30 am the following morning—and another "back-up" clock at 4:45 am in case the first one failed (substantiating my Type A personality). On weekends, I slept in—generally getting up as late as 5:00 or 5:30 am—so as to continue to chip away at my goals, *every day*. In essence, I worked an hour or an hour and a half nearly every morning, first thing, before the vast majority of the nation's alarm clocks had gone off. I once heard a marketing guru, Gary Bencivenga, refer to this as "Your Hour of Power," a key to massive success in any field, and over the years came to realize that I was not alone in this practice.

I learned that Apple's Tim Cook often rises at 3:45 am to start his day, Lewis Reeves, founder of Viga and formerly their chief executive officer, wakes at 4:30 am, and the alarm of James Constantinou, chief executive officer of Prestige Pawnbrokers, goes off at 4:45 am. In fact, the list of highly successful people, past and present, who woke/wake up early to work on their craft and improve their performance (professional golfers Gary Player and Tiger Woods, for example) is staggering! The earliest riser, however, was a guy by the name of Bill Gates (☺), who set his alarm during his college years at 1:30 am. This allowed him to learn computer programming on a giant mainframe computer at a nearby university that was not being used between 2:00 and 6:00 am. A coincidence? I don't think so. Somewhere, along the way, they learned one of the greatest secrets of success. "Early to bed and early to rise, makes one healthy, wealthy, and wise." Essentially, they do what's most important *first thing* that day.

As for me, the practice or approach has been enormously rewarding—beyond my wildest dreams! Virtually all of my professional goals have been accomplished, and then some, including my goal to write or edit a book that others could learn from (accomplished 1984). Indeed, this particular book (*GPS for Success*), one that I believe will have the most significant impact by far, reiterates that "success doesn't happen by chance."

THE "VALUE" OF MAKING LISTS IN ACTIVATING YOUR SUBCONSCIOUS MIND

Relative to time management, productivity, happiness, and goals, here are a few *life-changing lists* you can start writing immediately, to focus on during periods of downtime.

1. Long-term specific goals (e.g., losing 20 pounds over the next 15 months, exercising regularly to improve your aerobic fitness, writing a book or applying for a funded research grant, becoming a member or, better yet, a committee chair of a professional organization, or doubling your annual income within the next 2 years). I carry a notecard with me, listing my goals that I'm constantly looking at throughout the day. CRITICALLY IMPORTANT: Establish a major or *breakthrough goal* that would represent a *quantum leap* for you and your career (#1 priority)—and work on it every day until you achieve it. Then, establish a new breakthrough goal.

2. Write your six most important goals for tomorrow and prioritize them (called Vertical Planning). Start with the harder tasks, that is, the ones you perceive are more difficult.

3. Listing the things that you are most grateful for (good health, supportive family or spouse, travel opportunities, working with positive people who you consider good friends and esteemed colleagues). Why? *Being grateful for what you have leads you to attract and create more things to be grateful for.* Learn to appreciate yourself, your accomplishments, and the great things around you every day. Don't put off being happy, waiting for something wonderful to happen.

   Don't wait for good fortune; CREATE IT!

In summary, don't underestimate the power of setting goals in writing, visualizing and regularly affirming them, and doing something each day that moves you closer toward achieving those goals. Always have a major or breakthrough goal that you are working on!

As Joseph Murphy stated in his book, *The Power of Your Subconscious Mind*:

> Once you learn to contact and release the hidden power of your subconscious mind, you can bring into your life more power, more wealth, more happiness, and joy. You don't need to acquire this power. You already possess it.

Recognize that your subconscious mind is a powerful magnet for bringing goals and desires into your life. Whatever goal you give to your subconscious mind, it will work 24/7 to achieve. To activate it, simply write your goals down, visualize and affirm them each day, and see them as a brightening light at the end of a tunnel that you are constantly moving toward by taking action to achieve, every day. The bottom line? Written goals are like magnets. They pull us toward them. They are a commitment to do—and set the subconscious mind to work to achieve them.

However, caution is advised:

> You (the person you see in the mirror each day) have the single greatest influence on your destiny. Re-read the above-referenced passages. Following them can turn dreams into reality—on a regular basis. Tell your family, friends, and esteemed colleagues about your aspirations, to gain their support, but not your fiercest competitors. Remember the tremendous power that lies in the science of daily thought, repetition, and positive action. You will do what you once thought was impossible. Your GPS will guide you to your goals or destination. It cannot be otherwise.

I am the master of my fate, I am the captain of my soul.

Henley

6

Be Proactive: Just Do It!

What we think, or what we know, or what we believe, is in the end, of little consequence. The only thing of consequence is what we do.

Philosopher and philanthropist John Ruskin

Information and knowledge are not power; they are only potential power. It's what you *do (how you act)* with the knowledge that counts.

Entrepreneur, success guru John Assaraf

Oftentimes, the hardest part of any job is starting it. But experience tells us that once you actually start the job, the task wasn't anywhere near as bad as you thought it would be. *Action cures fear and procrastination.* Don't worry if it's not perfect. Ernest Hemingway, the American novelist and short story writer, who was awarded the Nobel Prize for Literature in 1954, woke up each morning and began writing. Why? Because he felt that his willpower and creativity tended to be higher earlier in the day. Similarly, the late Louis L'Amour was one of the best-selling authors of all time. His books consisted primarily of Western novels; however, he also wrote historical fiction, poetry, and short stories. Nearly 260 million copies of his books are in print worldwide, and every one of his more than 100 books remains in print. Still not impressed? More than two dozen films were adapted from L'Amour's novels and short stories! When asked the key to his prolific writing style, he responded, "*Start writing, no matter what. The water doesn't flow until the faucet is turned on.*" The bottom line? Take action!

DOI: 10.4324/9781003260387-8

THE ONLY PRODUCTIVITY TIP YOU'LL EVER NEED: START THE JOB!

The willingness to *start the job* is the littlest thing in life that makes the biggest difference. In fact, it's more important to start than to succeed. How can that be?! Because if you don't start the job, succeeding at it is virtually impossible.

AN INSIGHTFUL CONVERSATION ATOP AN ICEBERG

On a beautiful day, five penguins were sitting on an iceberg. The first penguin said, "Wow, the water looks wonderful today. I think I may go swimming later on." The second penguin said, "That's the clearest water I've ever seen. I bet it's really refreshing." The third penguin commented, "Well, if you go in swimming later on, maybe I'll go with you." The fourth penguin added, "What a spectacular day. I'll bet it would be really, really nice, going into the water for a swim." But it was the fifth penguin that got my attention. He said, "Hell, I'm going in." We've got too many people today sitting on their own iceberg: "Hmmm, I might do that," or "Maybe I'll do this." The person who takes the leap is invariably the one who is rewarded.

CURING PROCRASTINATION BY OVERCOMING INERTIA: START THE JOB!

Procrastination is opportunity's assassin.

American entrepreneur and TV spokesman Victor Kiam

Oftentimes, what overwhelms us is not the job itself; it's thinking about how hard it's going to be. One of the keys in achieving success is overcoming inertia. *Simply start the task.* That's the cure for procrastination. Author and management consultant Keith Ellis summed it up best when he said:

Inertia is the single greatest barrier to success. It's also the easiest to overcome. All you have to do is act. Any action you take, no matter how trivial, will do the trick. The easier you make it on yourself to act, the easier it is to overcome inertia. Focus on a single step, the smallest step you can think of. The moment you take action—any action—you will conquer inertia.

Similarly, Albert Einstein once said, "Nothing happens until something moves." Although he was speaking of science, he might just as well have been referring to getting things done. Most people are imprisoned by inertia. The only way to break free is to do something.

Avoid procrastination. Adopt the attitude, "Do it now." Why? Taking action provides three key benefits: It gets you started; it prevents a backlog, and it builds momentum. Once you've overcome inertia (body no longer at rest), you develop momentum, and it's much easier to keep going and get the job done.

Whenever I've got a big job, for example, writing a research grant, scientific report, or book chapter, I simply tell myself that I've just got to act on it by behaving in a certain way. Specifically, I've got to write a paragraph or two on it *today*. Just start—do something, even if it's poorly written—since it will be much easier to work on the next day, to refine and expand on my previous effort and begin to develop momentum. Scott Adams, creator of the popular comic strip *Dilbert*, states that his goals are best achieved by adopting a set of behaviors that regularly move him in a particular direction (toward his aspirations and dreams). That way, he succeeds every time he applies these behaviors.

When I give selected talks, I may hold up a copy of one of my books, sometimes with a $10 bill (my bookmark) hanging out, and ask the audience, "Who would like a free copy of my book. It is here for the taking." Lots of hands go up ... but typically everyone just remains in their seat for a long while. Finally, one brave soul will get it, both figuratively and literally, and actually walk up to me at the front of the auditorium, standing behind the podium, and take the book from my hand. I then ask the audience what did he/she (mentioning their name) do that no one else did? They got off their ass and moved in the direction of something they wanted. It seems to get the point across. That's the person who is successful. You don't just raise your hand, suggesting you are interested. *You take action!* People who routinely take action to achieve their wants, goals, and desires are the most successful. Period! Indeed, there's an enduring axiom that says, "The universe rewards action." Yet as simple as this principle is, it's surprising how many people get bogged down in analyzing, planning, and organizing when all they really need to do is take action. *Be a doer, not a talker.*

According to Harry Lorayne, the world's leading expert on mind training, "positive thoughts must become positive actions [which he referred to as positive doing] to accomplish anything worthwhile." As a matter of fact, spending all your time thinking positively isn't going to leave much time for accomplishing your goals and aspirations. In a nutshell, visualize the final outcome that you desire, and see yourself doing the actions to get you there. Then, DO IT! Recognize there will likely be unanticipated challenges along the way. Nevertheless, learning to accomplish something you've never done before, even if not perfect, will improve your skills and abilities to more adeptly navigate around future obstacles that you will encounter. Also, if you recognize that obstacles, more often than not, become "steppingstones" to achieving your lofty goals, you'll learn to welcome them.

AN ITALIAN MOTHER'S ADVICE TO HER SON

Former New York governor Mario Cuomo once said that his mother gave him two watchwords for success: "cerebral" and "physical," respectively.

1. Figure out exactly what it is you want to do; and,
2. Do it!

"JUST DO IT": THE ARTHUR L. WILLIAMS, JR. MOTTO

Billionaire executive Arthur L. Williams, Jr., who early in his career aspired to be a professional football coach, decided he wanted to do more with his life and made his fortune by selling life insurance and through investments. Although many people said he had none of the common requisites for achieving overwhelming success in life, I'd strongly disagree. Two reasons. When Williams' father died suddenly of a heart attack, his whole-life insurance policy left their family woefully underinsured. Art learned about and championed a much-needed option for life insurance, called "term insurance," as a less expensive alternative to paying whole-life insurance premiums. And, he advised the masses to invest the difference in cost (i.e., savings)! His slogan became, "Buy Term and Invest the Difference." Indeed, he convinced countless customers to switch from their conventional whole-life insurance to term policies. Art also had the mindset to make it big in whatever field he chose to pursue.

The Williams philosophy?

> You can beat 50 percent of the people in America simply by working hard (i.e., outworking the competition). You beat another 40 percent by being a person of honesty and integrity and standing for something (starting to sound familiar?). However, the last 10 percent is a dogfight in the free enterprise system, because you're likely competing with others who have the same philosophy.

Williams' approach to business embraced three pillars: Inspire others; treat people like gold; and "Just do it"! He emphasized that your life is a direct result of what you DO—not necessarily what you say you're going to do. *One of the most motivational/inspirational talks I've ever heard is Williams' "Just Do It," first presented in 1987—a must see (available on the Internet).* With his coaching background, he also exemplified many of the success principles and mindsets that are discussed in *GPS for Success*. Indeed, the above-referenced talk and one of his books, entitled *All You Can Do Is All You Can Do, But All You Can Do Is Enough* (*New York Times* Best-seller, 1988) had a profound and favorable impact on me and my early career direction. Three of the most powerful Williams quotes that stayed with me over the years are listed here:

- "To win you must pay the price. If you haven't won, you haven't paid the price."
- "Almost is a way of life for almost everybody."

- "I'm not telling you it is going to be easy—I'm telling you it's going to be worth it."

JUST

DO

IT.

Nike*

TOMMY HOPKINS—A SALES LEGEND

Since 1976, Tommy Hopkins has dedicated himself to providing the finest sales training strategies and techniques to individuals and companies alike. He truly is a "rags to riches" story, who made it big in real estate and training salespeople in all walks of life.

His tagline? *"My goal is your success."* He emphasized that the key to successful sales is the "D word," and it goes far beyond "Desire." No, the key word is *"Discipline"*—which encompasses the things you must do to achieve your sales goals and dreams (e.g., establish trust, be competitive, follow up with your customers with regular communications, exceed people's expectations, and stand behind the products you represent).

Hopkins, in his seminars, established "The Law of GOYA" as a cardinal tenet of sales success.

"Get Off Your Ass"

This simple law is very effective. You have to do something every day that moves you closer toward your goals and dreams. Just be in action!

THE ULTIMATE SUCCESS SECRET?

The *Harvard Business Review* once reprinted the insightful letterhead used by a large corporation. The message contained herein may just represent the ultimate secret of success:

---

* Although there is controversy regarding the origin of the famous Nike logo, copyrighted in 1988, I found it ironic that the great talk by Art Williams, "Just Do It," was first presented a year earlier, in 1987.

To look is one thing. To see what you look at is another. To understand what you see is a third. To learn from what you understand is still something else. But *to act* on what you learn is all that really matters.

Nearly 20 years ago, I read a wonderful book by Daniel S. Kennedy entitled *The Ultimate Success Secret*. Kennedy, who described himself as an author-speaker-consultant, made it his business to surround himself with exceptionally successful individuals, in all walks of life, and to study them in zealous search of the #1 or ultimate success secret. What initially got my attention, in addition to the catchy title, was the book cover, which posed the question: *Is it possible that there is one single, super powerful secret of success of far greater importance than all others?* Indeed, a multitude of authors, researchers, psychologists, behavioral scientists, efficiency experts, and self-help gurus have pondered this question.

From a historical perspective, in 1917, America's first billionaire, Andrew Carnegie, sent Napoleon Hill on a mission to discover the most common behavioral characteristics shared by the most exceptional achievers of their time. Eventually, Hill came up with 13 such principles, followed by Stephen Covey's blockbuster best-selling book detailing *The 7 Habits of Highly Successful People*. Motivational guru, the late Zig Ziglar, identified "Ten Qualities" of highly successful people in "his quest for superiority over all the rest." But in Daniel Kennedy's *The Ultimate Success Secret*, he had the chutzpah (i.e., audacity, nerve) to boil it down to a "single secret of success," above all other success strategies, universally practiced and relied on by virtually all extraordinarily successful individuals. And, in contrast to approaches emphasized by Napoleon Hill and others, Kennedy focused less attention on the thinking of highly successful people and paid a lot more attention to their behavior.

In his extensive research, Kennedy noted that a constant, universal characteristic of movie or big screen heroes is their bias for *action* (e.g., Superman, Spiderman, Action Jackson, Rocky 1, 2 ...). He also highlighted the fact that the only antidote for worry or concern is *action*. And, when reviewing a number of highly successful individuals who overcame physical, appearance, and/or medical challenges, the common denominator was positive attitudes and *actions*. For example, Kennedy shared the story of John and Greg Rice, who were imprisoned by their midget size until they met Glen Turner, author of *Dare to be Great*, who convinced them that even "little men" could do big things. John and Greg became very popular (even famous ☺), well-paid, motivational speakers on the topic "Thinking Big"—even though they had to climb on a table so the audience could see them! Public speaking complemented their countless TV and movie appearances (visibility leads to opportunities) and highly successful real estate sales and investment business.

Kennedy emphasized that for every handicap, obstacle, and tragedy in life, there are two outcomes or stories. In Story #1, unfortunately the most common, those afflicted will allow the handicap to imprison them, often diminishing their self-esteem, social network, annual income, well-being, quality of life, and even their health. Whereas in Story #2, the individual accomplishes the most extraordinary things in spite of the handicap or challenges they are facing, increasing their happiness, success, and physical and mental well-being, by embracing a *purpose-driven life*. In fact, highly successful people may often capitalize on their handicap, as John and Greg Rice did. Each individual, by his or her attitude and, more importantly, actions, chooses which outcome will be theirs.

THE CURIOUS LINK BETWEEN EARLY POVERTY AND SUBSEQUENT WEALTH

The Story #1–Story #2 analogy also pertains to ultimate wealth— sometimes enormous wealth. While it is true that countless economically deprived children will remain disadvantaged throughout their entire lives (Story #1), others will gravitate to middle-to-upper socioeconomic status as adults, or in some cases, enormous wealth (Story #2). Indeed, many of today's multi-millionaires and billionaires grew up in families of lower socioeconomic status and even poverty conditions.

My review of the early days of some of the wealthiest people on the planet, including Oprah Winfrey, Howard Schultz, Ralph Lauren, Kenneth Langone, Sheldon Adelson, J.K. Rowling, LeBron James, George Soros, and Jeff Bezos, revealed unexpected and sobering findings. Some reported not having running water or electricity at times during their childhood, or not having enough money to buy new clothes. Another lived for years in government-subsidized housing. Others weren't sure where they would be sleeping (sometimes in a car) or, for that matter, where their next meal was coming from. A 16-year-old mother and deadbeat dad were breadwinners for another family. Yet another multi-millionaire, who grew up in a depressing inner-city environment, said "with my background, I should not be where I am today." Virtually all acknowledged, in one way or another, during their growing-up years, that their families focused on or were fighting about *money*, because they had none. Clearly, all resolved, either consciously or unconsciously, that a major life goal would be to NOT emulate the penniless early years that they experienced with their own families. Accordingly, it seems that all became preoccupied, perhaps even obsessed, with making money, big money, and via the "law of attraction," ultimately gravitated to occupations they were passionate about where this was possible. These included: entrepreneurship, computer science, investment, real estate, entertainment, clothing, high school/college athletics as a gateway to professional sports, and, yes—even writing. ☺

In essence, those who were economically deprived as children and adolescents and remained so throughout life conformed to their situation by believing that this was simply their destiny (Story #1), as characterized by their actions or, more appropriately, inaction. On the other hand, others with similar early experiences chose to defy their situation with unwavering goals, positive thought, visualization, affirmation, and massive action for a better life (Story #2). They chose to aggressively pursue and live the life that they imagined.

Another inspirational story, illustrating *The Ultimate Success Secret*, described by Dan Kennedy, pertained to the creation of a bustling catalog business that initially focused on women's clothing accessories.

Take Action when your "Inner Voice" Speaks. At age 24, an expectant mother, Lillian Vernon, took out a small advertisement in the September 1951 issue of *Seventeen Magazine* for $495, offering a personalized handbag, monogrammed with the customer's initials, for $2.99 plus tax and a belt for $1.99. She used Vernon Specialties as the company name. Lillian believed in her idea and acted on it, even though $495 was a great deal of money at the time, and she had no market research or business experience to support her venture. Nevertheless, she proved to be a visionary. The advertisement generated $32,000 in orders, and her business began to thrive. Subsequently, the Lillian Vernon Corporation was founded in 1965, went public in 1987, and was the first company to be founded by a woman to be publically traded on the American Stock Exchange. In its heyday, the business had nine catalogs, online marketing, and a website, with yearly revenues approaching $300 million. The moral of the story? Lillian Vernon *took massive action* to support her idea of what clothing accessories women wanted, often even before they knew. In doing so, she pioneered a thriving new business—and made millions along the way.

THE LOBSTER AND THE ROCK: AN EXAMPLE NOT TO EMULATE

Dr. Orison Swett Marden was an American inspirational author who wrote about achieving success in life and founded *Success Magazine* in 1897. His writings, including many famous quotes, discuss relevant principles, practices, and behavior skills that make for a fulfilling, purposeful, highly successful life. One of my favorites, shown here, highlights the antithesis of this chapter:

> A lobster, when left high and dry among the rocks, does not have the sense enough to work his way back to the sea, but waits for the sea to come to him. If it does not come, he remains where he is and dies, although the slightest effort would enable him to reach the waves, which are perhaps within a yard of him. The world is full of human lobsters; people stranded on the rocks of indecision and procrastination, who, instead of putting forth their own energies, are waiting for some grand billow of good fortune to set them afloat.
>
> **Orison Swett Marden**

I chuckled when I first read this quotation, because it reminds me of a shortened, modified version that I've been telling my students and junior colleagues for many years now:

> Don't wait for your ship to come in. Swim out to it by taking action to achieve your goals in life.

In summary, action is the foundational key to all success. *Imperfect action is better than perfect inaction.*

READY, FIRE: AIM

The quickest way to hit a target is to fire, see where the bullet landed, and then adjust your aim accordingly.
SATISFACTION COMES FROM ENOUGH ACTION

Epilogue

I have a colleague who has been talking for years about getting an advanced degree and additional training. It's been more than two decades now, and he still hasn't embarked on that advanced degree. His salary, job title, and professional status have remained essentially unchanged. If there is anything I've learned in the field of personal development, it is that there is a great void between *talkers* and *doers*. Had he gotten the advanced degree and continued his quest for a more fulfilling, purpose-driven life, I shudder to think how much more satisfying his professional career would have been today.

Are you pleased with your place in the world? If your answer is "yes," what's your next port of call? If your answer is "no," what are *you* going to do about it?
Earl Nightingale, *Earl Nightingale's Greatest Discovery,* **Dodd/Mead, Publisher**

In summary, Daniel Kennedy's single super powerful "secret of success" is TAKING ACTION, specifically MASSIVE ACTION, to achieve your goals, objectives, and desires. Ideas are worthless unless we *act* on them. Without question, he is correct! Why? After years of talking about the need for this book, and several previous starts and restarts, I finally decided to prioritize it as #1, took action nearly every day for many months to finish it, and it got done.☺

7

Be Persistent: Overcoming Setbacks That Line the Road to Success

Over, under, around, or through, whatever it takes I'll do.

Businessman, author, motivational speaker T. Harv Eker

For many years now, Professor Angela Duckworth and her associates at the University of Pennsylvania have been investigating the variables beyond intelligence and talent that predict future success. Their early studies found that the relation between self-discipline and achievement was twice as large as the relation between Intelligence Quotient (IQ) and achievement. Others have also reported that grit or resilience, that is, the capacity to return to a previous level of well-being after a period of adversity, was a greater predictor of success than IQ—suggesting that it mattered more than talent or skill. In aggregate, Duckworth's pioneering investigations found conclusive evidence that passion, *perseverance*, stamina, and how consistently you work in a direction over time are the strongest predictors of success. The fact of the matter is that highly successful people tend to *persevere*, self-regulate, and push themselves to success. They're also highly resilient, no matter what the goal.

Steve Jobs insightfully said: "I'm convinced that about half of what separates the successful entrepreneurs from the non-successful ones is pure perseverance." Indeed, the world is full of "could've beens"—people who had great ideas, aspirations, or inventions but who gave up before achieving their goals. And oftentimes, research suggests that they were closer to achieving them than they realized. *The bottom line? If you aren't willing to deal with setbacks and rejection, someone else will.* Winners in life continue to pursue their dreams and aspirations, even in

DOI: 10.4324/9781003260387-9

the face of adversity, working toward them day in and day out. Research from Marketing Wisdom suggests that approximately 80 percent of prospects decline a "proposal/ask" before eventually saying "Yes." Often, a negative reply or "no" means, "no, not right now," "no, I need to be even more convinced," "no, let me think about it" or "no, I need to feel more comfortable in working with you." In the interim, attempt to maintain regular visibility with them (visibility leads to opportunities) and build additional trust with the client by providing great service and timely responses, and exceeding their expectations whenever possible. Why? Because people have come to a sobering realization: When it comes to working with others, the past is generally prologue to the future.

In summary, rejection is inevitable. In fact, if you are not being regularly rejected, you are not asking enough! Remember, setbacks line the road to success. By recognizing the different meanings of the word "no," with the right strategies and responses, up to four out of five times, you can turn a "no" into a "yes." It's true—patience is a virtue. Remember, neither intelligence, socioeconomic status, good looks, a fabulous wardrobe, nor for that matter, even perfection, determines success—but persistence does. Persistence or perseverance pays.

The most successful people in the world have had countless failures. The key to success is how you respond to setbacks or disappointment. An exercise science student once asked me, "Aren't you Dr. Franklin? Wow! I've read many of your articles. How do you write all the books and research reports that you do?" He was surprised by my response. I said to him, "I'm the King of Rejection." He responded, "Excuse me?" I repeated, "I'm the King of Rejection. You don't see all the stuff I submit that gets rejected, or that reviewers/editors request major revision on. You only see the stuff that ultimately gets published. Persistence pays."

I love these "failure" anecdotes about some of our most treasured American and British products and icons:

- Thomas Edison said he had thousands of learning experiments before he invented the light bulb.
- Abraham Lincoln lost eight elections before becoming president.
- Colonel Sanders suffered more than a thousand rejections before he sold his first chicken recipe.
- Theodore Geisel (aka Dr. Seuss) had his first book turned down by 23 publishers.

- Authors of the best-selling *Chicken Soup for the Soul®* (Canfield/Hansen) approached 144 publishers with their book idea before one agreed to publish it.
- J.K. Rowling's *Harry Potter* book was rejected 12 times by publishers before one decided to take a gamble on it.
- Apple computers were turned down by both Atari and Hewlett-Packard.
- In 1905, the University of Bern rejected a PhD dissertation, characterizing it as "irrelevant and fanciful." The student who wrote it (Albert Einstein) eventually succeeded anyway.
- Babe Ruth struck out 1,330 times, but he also hit 714 home runs.
- Dance legend Fred Astaire received one of the most scathing screen test rejections in Hollywood history. The studio executive wrote: "Can't act. Slightly bald. Can dance a little."
- Actor Sylvester Stallone was, at one time, homeless, living in the Port Authority Bus Terminal in New York. While writing Rocky, he reportedly sold his dog to help pay the rent.

Thomas Watson, founder of IBM, was a pretty smart guy. He said, "The way to succeed is to double your failure rate." Hockey legend Wayne Gretzky put it this way, "You miss 100 percent of the shots you don't take."

I clipped this direct quote out of the newspaper—it was particularly enlightening, coming from the basketball superstar Michael Jordan. He said:

> I have missed more than 9,000 shots in my career. I have lost almost 300 games. On 26 occasions I was entrusted to take the game-winning shot and I missed. I have failed over and over again in my life. And that's precisely why I succeed.

LIFE SETBACKS: DON'T STAY DOWN WHEN YOU STUMBLE

Those referenced earlier experienced a multitude of consecutive setbacks and rejections on their way to overwhelming success! When you stumble, let it fuel your passion and commitment to succeed rather than derail your goals and aspirations. Don't empower those who reject or discourage you from achieving your dreams. Instead, muster up the discipline, determination, and persistence to prove them wrong.

"SPURS' TITLE IS A TESTAMENT TO PERSISTENCE"

Several years ago, June 16, 2014 to be exact, the above-referenced article, published in *The New York Times*, got my attention—so I read and saved it.

In a corner of the San Antonio Spurs' locker room, there was a framed quotation from the muckraking social reformer Jacob Riis that read:

> When nothing seems to help, I go back and look at the stonecutter hammering away at his rock perhaps a hundred times without as much as a crack showing in it. Yet at the hundred and first blow it will split in two, and I know it was not that blow that did it—but all that had gone before.

Because the Spurs had one of the most internationally represented rosters, Riis' words were translated into French, Spanish, and Portuguese on plaques that hung in the hall outside the locker room. If that doesn't clarify how important this message was to the team's core mission, then consider the name of one of Coach Gregg Popovich's own private wine labels: *Rock and Hammer.*

In a locker room soaked with an alcohol celebration late Sunday night after the Spurs beat the Miami Heat in five games, wrapping up their fifth N.B.A. championship in 15 seasons, there was special significance in Riis' motivational and foretelling quotation. The clinching victory, which came following an early 16-point deficit, and this season, which began with the lingering devastation of the previous season's collapse in the N.B.A. finals, were a substantiation of those virtues.

"Whenever I'm done with this game, that's going to be hanging up in my house for my kids to read the rest of my life," forward Matt Bonner said, taking a swig of beer and nodding at the framed quotation. "The lessons in that sign is why we can start out the way we did tonight and come back and win by 20 points—keep pounding the rock."

The take home message? Whether it pertains to winning basketball championships or achieving success in life, keep pounding the rock, because persistence pays! Get up after being knocked down, dust yourself off, take MASSIVE ACTION, and keep moving in the direction of your goals and dreams.

This quote from one of the most popular authors of our time got my attention:

I think it fair to say that by any conventional measure, a mere seven years after my graduation day, I had failed on an epic scale. An exceptionally short-lived marriage had imploded, and I was jobless, a lone parent, and as poor as it is possible to be in modern Britain without being homeless. The fears that my parents had had for me, and that I had had for myself, had both come to pass, and by every usual standard, I was the biggest failure I knew.

Now, I am not going to stand here and tell you that failure is fun. That period of my life was a dark one, and I had no idea that there was going to be what the press has since represented as a kind of fairy tale resolution. I had no idea then how far the tunnel extended, and for a long time, any light at the end of it was a hope rather than a reality.

So why do I talk about the benefits and failures? Simply because failure meant a stripping away of the inessential. I stopped pretending to myself that I was anything other than what I was and began to direct all my attention into finishing the one work that mattered to me. Had I really succeeded at anything else, I might never have found the determination to succeed in the one arena I believed I truly belonged. I was set free, because my greatest fear had been realized, and I was still alive, and I still had a daughter whom I adored, and I had an old typewriter and a big idea. And so rock bottom became the solid foundation on which I rebuilt my life.

You might never fail on the scale I did, but some failure in life is inevitable. It is impossible to live without failing at something, unless you live so cautiously that you might as well not have lived at all—in which case, you fail by default.

Failure gave me an inner security that I never attained by passing examinations. Failure taught me things about myself that I could have learned no other way. I discovered that I had a strong will and more discipline than I had suspected; I also found out that I had friends whose value was truly above the price of rubies.

The knowledge that you have emerged wiser and stronger from setbacks means that you are, ever after, secure in your ability to survive. You will never truly know yourself, or the strength of your relationships, until both have been tested by adversity.

Who was this speaker? J.K. Rowling, creator of the beloved *Harry Potter* series. These words were excerpted from her commencement address at Harvard University in 2008 (http://news.harvard.edu/gazette/story/2008 /06/text-of-j-k-rowling-speech/).

STRATEGIES TO MAINTAIN AND ENHANCE PERSISTENCE TO ACHIEVE YOUR GOALS

- Embrace President Clinton's 1992 presidential campaign theme song, "Don't Stop Thinking About Tomorrow," by the British-American rock band Fleetwood Mac.
- Envision "persistence as the pathway" to success.
- Start the job (no matter what), keep "moving" in the direction of your goals, and break down bigger goals into smaller, manageable pieces.
- Maintain a laser focus on all of your goals, which should be WRITTEN. Define your goals precisely and exactly. Goals should be visualized and affirmed daily; repeated affirmations should be statements you say to yourself out loud—"I am going to spend an hour or more today on writing the introduction for my grant proposal." Prioritize major, breakthrough, life-changing goals (which take lots of time [sometimes years]) as ones you should be devoting time to every day.
- Focus daily on the underlying reasons or rationale for your breakthrough goals. Zero in on the *whys* other than yourself (e.g., parents, spouse, children, students, colleagues, helping or filling a needed service for lots of people, people you don't even know, and filling that void). Why? Because we will generally do more for others than we will do for ourselves. For example, when J.K. Rowling was living on government assistance in the United Kingdom, she wanted not just to survive but to thrive. Her motivation to finish her first

Harry Potter book was fueled, in large part, by the need to support a beautiful little girl she was now raising alone.

- If I've learned anything as a healthcare provider over the past four decades, it's that much of the deterioration in cognitive and bodily function that is commonly attributed to aging is actually due to disuse and unhealthy lifestyle habits. By improving your lifestyle and risk factor profile (regular exercise, healthy nutrition [six or more servings of fruits/veggies every day], moderate or no alcohol consumption, stop cigarette smoking, 7–8 hours of sleep per night, avoid addictive drugs, and don't sweat the small stuff), you can attenuate the aging process and decrease the likelihood of chronic disease. Consider that regular exercise (e.g., brisk walking) reduces your risk of a heart attack by up to 50 percent—as does cutting your cholesterol level by 40 points. Stopping cigarette smoking in your 30s or younger can add 10–12 years to your lifespan! Avoid breathing other people's cigarette smoke (i.e., secondhand smoke), which increases the risk of heart disease by 30 percent. Finally, watch your weight. If your body mass index is over 35, you are in the highest risk group for developing chronic diseases and dying prematurely.

- *Major health problems in your 40s, 50s, and 60s, which are largely preventable, can derail a promising career.* By embracing aggressive lifestyle changes, you can effectively "turn back time" so that you have the energy, mental acuity, and functional reserves to continue to vigorously and passionately pursue your career well into the golden years. Research shows an undeniable link between healthy lifestyle and high achievement. A study in the *Journal of Labor Research* found that regular exercisers earn 9 percent higher salaries than their less active counterparts. Many of the most successful companies in the world, including Google, have on-site exercise facilities. Think about it. Achieving health goals sets the stage for other accomplishments to fall into place. People begin to think, "wow, if I can do that, maybe I can achieve this goal too."

Trivia: Walt Disney, who was a heavy smoker with an infamous cough, died of lung cancer at age 65. Chesterfield and Camels were his favorites.

- Avoid the common mistake of "instant gratification," and realize that achieving your breakthrough goals only occurs with constant effort over long periods of time. According to a widely cited study by Stanford University researchers, children who were able to wait 15 minutes before gobbling up a marshmallow were rewarded with a second one that had been promised. During adolescence, those who embraced delayed gratification were more likely to excel academically and professionally.

- See new (i.e., not yet achieved) breakthrough goals as being analogous to another breakthrough goal that you previously attained and that was well worth it, providing great dividends and extraordinary opportunities for many subsequent years (e.g., getting my PhD at Penn State University in 1976—which took 5+ years) continues to bear fruit to this day!

- Recognize that you recharge persistence with consistency rather than intensity of work (1 hour per day, every day, is superior to 5 hours on a Saturday).

- Make the commitment, and share it with supportive friends, colleagues, and family, and stick it out until you reach the goal or objective.

- Realize that maintaining persistence, to devote time each day to *your goals*, will require sacrifice. Finding time each day for them will necessitate giving up other things that should not compromise health, reading, continuing education, important professional or family commitments, rest, and recreation (R & R) days, and vacation time. Use your entitled R & R days and vacation time, which have been shown to recharge, rejuvenate, and ultimately increase productivity.

According to the Billionaire Census published by market research firm Wealth-X, the majority of billionaires in the world were self-made. Many had limited education, were of lower socioeconomic status growing up, and were of average intelligence. Their secret? They found something they were good at and loved to do, worked harder than most, remained focused, and maintained the passion and persistence to achieve their goals.

12 QUOTES ON WHY PERSISTENCE IS CRITICAL FOR SUCCESS

Energy and persistence conquer all things.

Benjamin Franklin

Nothing in this world can take the place of persistence. Nothing is more common than unsuccessful men with talent. Persistence and determination alone are omnipotent.

Calvin Coolidge

Patience, persistence, and perspiration make an unbeatable combination for success.

Napoleon Hill

Success is the result of perfection, hard work, learning from failure, loyalty, and persistence.

Colin Powell

You may encounter many defeats, but you must not be defeated.

Maya Angelou

Ambition is the path to success. Persistence is the vehicle you arrive in.

Bill Bradley

Paralyze resistance with persistence.

Woody Hayes

If you are going through hell, keep going.

Winston Churchill

Champions keep playing until they get it right.

Billie Jean King

Being at the right place at the right time, always favors the persistent person.

Mort Crim

If you can't fly, then run, if you can't run then walk, if you can't walk then crawl, but whatever you do you have to keep moving forward.

Martin Luther King, Jr.

Why is it that some people seemed to be destined to succeed at whatever they do, whereas others are prone to underachievement and failure? The answer is all about mindset. You don't get to be one of those successful people for nothing. There's not room for everybody at the top. If you want to rise above, to reach the peak of the mountain and reap the glory that goes with it, then climb. And don't stop climbing til you get there.

Venessa Thiele

The message here is perhaps best captured in the final two quotes, that is, those by Drs. King, Jr., and Thiele, respectively. If you want to go from where you are to where you want to be, you've got to keep (i.e., by taking action) moving toward your ultimate goal or destination. The critical role of persistence or perseverance is apparent.

In summary, time and time again, the most successful companies and careers have proven that *failure is the life blood of innovation*, and *mistakes are the portals of discovery*. Bottom line? Embrace setbacks to motivate you to take MASSIVE ACTIONS that will ensure your future success.

I think Dolly Parton beautifully captured the essence of life's setbacks when she said: "If you want the rainbow, you've got to put up with the rain." ☺

READY TO "GIVE UP"?

Next time you are "down," overwhelmed by yet another setback, go to the internet and listen to the "Top 5 Most Epic Inspiring Speeches That Will Set You Up for Success" Goalcast. The inspirational experiences and perspective of Rudy Francisco, William McRaven, Inky Johnson, Rock Thomas, and Arnold Schwarzenegger will, without question, reinvigorate your willingness to persist during your most difficult times and devastating setbacks. I guarantee it!

8

Be Someone Who Asks for What You Want: Reject Rejection

You've got to ask! Asking is, in my opinion, the world's most powerful- and neglected-secret to success and happiness.

Philanthropist, columnist, multi-millionaire Percy Ross

Jesus said, in his Sermon on the Mount, "Ask and it shall be given to you." How true it is! Jack Canfield and Mark Victor Hansen wrote an entire book, *The Aladdin Factor*, about this topic. I highly recommend it! In it, they contend that one of the greatest lessons you'll ever learn is how to ask for what you want in life.

Over the years, I've witnessed so many good friends and esteemed colleagues appointed to committees, writing groups, consulting opportunities, invited lectures, and prestigious boards—some were paid, whereas others were not. When I asked them, "How the heck did you get that wonderful opportunity?" they invariably said, "I contacted the director or committee chair and *asked*, and he/she offered me the appointment." Don't assume people can read your mind. *Ask for what you want in life.*

Years ago, during a casual conversation with the executive vice president of a major professional organization that I'd been a member of for decades, including serving as a past-president, he commented that I'd done virtually everything possible for this professional association. I responded that my only disappointment was that I'd never been asked to give one of the "keynote" lectures for their annual meeting. A few months later, the Program Committee ironically contacted me and

DOI: 10.4324/9781003260387-10

asked if I would be willing to give one of their two major lectures at the annual meeting before ~5,000 attendees, which included generous compensation. Was this a coincidence? I don't think so, as I had mentioned the unattained goal months earlier, and that I was interested in the opportunity. Somehow, that information got back to one of the key organizational decision-makers, the president-elect, whose call it was to select this named lecturer.

A telling statistic from the marketing world. Herbert True, a marketing specialist at Notre Dame University, reported that 44 percent of all salespeople quit trying after the first call. They hear, "We're not interested in your product," and the salesperson never goes back. An additional 24 percent quit after the second call, 14 percent quit after the third call, and another 12 percent quit trying to sell to their prospect after the fourth rejection. That means 94 percent of all salespeople quit after the fourth call. But 60 percent of all sales are made *after* the fourth call. Ask, ask, ask, ask, ask, until they tell you, "Never come back again." I've seen it time and time again where a sales agent will show up a fourth or fifth time, and a staff member quietly says, "You know, this guy's been here several times previously. Let's give him a small order and see how he does."

In his phenomenal book *Ask More, Get More*, Michael Alden says that too many times, whether it be negotiating the price of a car or asking for a raise, people leave money on the table. His point: "Ask for more, and you'll get more. It's not greed. It's getting what you deserve."

So, what do you do when you're negotiating, trying to get more for yourself, but they say, "Well, we can't do that." Follow Alden's advice, and simply reply, "Why not?" That puts them in an uncomfortable defensive posture, and more often than not, they'll positively respond to your request by sweetening the deal.

It's also appropriate to say, "Well, is there anything else that you can do for me?" My wife does that all the time, and I'm always amazed that they'll respond with something like, "Well, yes, we can give you another $100 off." I've done this myself when negotiating 3-year car leases, getting $5 to $8 reductions in my monthly payments, getting free oil changes my first 6 to 12 months, or both.

It's so simple. Always ask "Why can't you do that?" Ask, "Is there anything else that you can do for me?" The fact of the matter is, they can almost always do more for you. *But you must ask.*

ASK QUESTIONS TO AVOID ARGUMENTS

Willard Sloan wrote an article entitled, "Arguments Don't Win Friends," highlighting the fact that one should be extremely careful when embarking on a heated discussion that's likely to evolve into a serious argument that does not allow the person you strongly disagree with to save face. Rather than telling them, especially in front of others, that their statement or contention is "wrong" or "inaccurate," the best way to avoid an argument is to simply ask questions. All you need to say is, "Why do you say that?" or "How do you know that?" or simply "Why is that?" This approach puts the burden of proof squarely on the shoulders of the person who made the statement that you feel is wrong, inaccurate, or unjustified. Instead of trying to prove the commenter wrong, you essentially put him or her on the defensive, forcing them to prove the merits of their statement or discredit themselves accordingly. Using this approach, you come out of it looking professional, wise, calm, and level-headed, and every so often, the other person's contention proves to be correct—allowing *you* to save face.

ASK FOR THE COMPENSATION YOU DESERVE

In Daniel Kennedy's outstanding book *The Ultimate Success Secret*, he addresses the value hang-up that so many of us have regarding our fees and prices for talks, consulting, or services rendered to potential clients. Years ago, I remember being contacted by a small Midwest university who asked me to serve as a visiting professor there for 1 week, giving numerous talks to the students and faculty as well as the community. In addition, several Q/A sessions were planned with university administrators, faculty, and students. I learned that the visiting professorship was made possible via a $10,000 educational grant from a generous University alumnus. When asked what I would require to serve in this role, I requested that my driving mileage, hotel, and meals be covered, along with an $8,000 honorarium, held my breath, and thought to myself, "Wow, Franklin, you've got a lot of nerve asking for $1,600 a day! Who do you think you are — a rock star?" But the sobering realization I came to understand is that clients (who ask for your services) largely accept your appraisal of your value, and most people tend to under-value and underprice the services they provide. The University responded—OK—we look forward to having you with us for this annual event.

In 2018, I was invited to serve as a visiting professor at University Tor Vergata in Rome, Italy, for a 2-month tenure. I accepted the appointment with a compensation of €12,000 (before taxes), understanding that my teaching commitment would be just 2 hours/week over the duration of my faculty position. Despite several hours each week in preparation, it was, living in central Rome, literally 5 minutes from the Vatican, the opportunity of a lifetime—and reinforced the notion that if your specific services are requested your expertise may be generously compensated, well beyond what I thought I was worth.

ASK FOR THE SALE OR DONATION— THEN STOP TALKING

All great salespeople have one thing in common — enthusiasm for their product or their cause. Nevertheless, if you don't ask your customer or prospect for the sale or donation, respectively, the answer is always "no." Relative to sales, consider your brief sales pitch from the customer's point of view—first, find out what matters to them. There is also nothing wrong with sharing a small negative on the product, which gives you (the salesperson) added credibility. A study published in the *Journal of Consumer Research* showed that buyers were more likely to purchase a product when they were told about a minor problem with it. Finally, using an emphatic curse word to convey greater conviction or persuasiveness can sometimes be helpful. "Excuse my language, but this is a damn good product that our family has used for years." Once you've helped a potential client understand the value of a particular product, or the purpose of a fundraiser, ask for the sale ("Would you like to buy it?") or for the donation ("Would you like to donate?"). THEN BE QUIET. DON'T UTTER A SOUND! This rule applies whether you are in a face-to-face meeting or on the phone. If you remain quiet, the customer or prospect is much more likely to answer with a "Yes!"

We usually say too much. It makes us less persuasive.
Marketing/management guru Katya Andresen

Question: Why did you give?

Answer: Because I was asked.

Famous fundraising saying

ASK FOR THINGS YOU WANT: THE MAGIC OF A FACE-TO-FACE MEETING

Getting into Graduate School. When I graduated from Kent State University in 1970 with a bachelor's degree in Health and Physical Education, I decided to immediately pursue a master's degree at a preeminent academic institution of higher learning, that is, the University of Michigan. There was just one problem—I graduated from Kent State with a C⁺ grade point average (GPA), and everyone told me "there's no way in hell" you are going to get into Michigan with that pathetic GPA.

I agreed that it would be challenging, to say the least—and knew that the conventional application process (submit formal letter, send academic transcripts, wait) would be very unlikely to result in my being accepted at Michigan. So, I came up with an ingenious, unconventional plan to achieve a breakthrough goal that I desperately wanted, an approach that I've continued to use to this day.

I contacted a key professor of exercise science/physiology at the University of Michigan, the chairman of the department, told him I was interested in obtaining my master's degree under his mentorship, and asked for a face-to-face meeting. And, to make it difficult for him to turn me down, I lied, telling him that I'd be spending a good portion of my summer with family in the Ann Arbor area (I had no family there). He responded that he was off during the summer but would be in the office for 2 days during the month of July. We confirmed a date, time, and meeting place—the meeting was on!

In preparation for the meeting, I read several of the professor's published papers and identified his professional areas of interest. The day of the appointment, I set two alarm clocks to wake up very early and proceeded to drive the 4 hours it took to reach Ann Arbor from my home in Cleveland, Ohio. I arrived at his office nearly 30 minutes ahead of time, well-groomed, clean shaven, wearing a conservative sport coat, white shirt, blue tie, and black socks. My loafer shoes were carefully shined the night before. I greeted him with a smile and a firm handshake and maintained good posture and eye contact during our hour-long meeting that day (which was longer than I had anticipated). I'm glad I had done my homework—since oftentimes during our discussions I was able to cite papers he had written that were particularly insightful to me and my research interests.

I vividly remember his closing statement to me that day: "Barry, I enjoyed meeting with you today, and your passion for the field is apparent. However, I must be frank with you; your GPA is considerably below the level that is normally required to get into the University of Michigan." My reply? "Yes, professor—I realized that my overall GPA is low, at least by Michigan's high standards, but if you carefully review my grades the final year at Kent, they were, in fact, compatible with your admission criteria." And, looking at him face-to-face, I closed the conversation by stating that, "If I'm fortunate enough to be accepted at the University of Michigan, under your direction, you will not be disappointed in my performance— I'll not only meet but will exceed your expectations." As I left his office that day, I thanked him profusely for his time and consideration. This was reinforced by a thank you card I had already purchased—which I inscribed immediately after the meeting with a generous handwritten note, expressing my appreciation and gratitude for the time he had spent with me that day, and mailed it (in Ann Arbor). I drove back to Cleveland and reflected on the positive meeting that we had had. Then I waited, several months, for the decision letter to come in the mail from the Rackham Graduate School.

Despite the plethora of naysayers, including friends, family, and even former (undergraduate) professors, who all said I would likely not be accepted at Michigan, I remained cautiously optimistic—and I'm glad I did (another bona fide success strategy—think about your goal often and see it coming to fruition). The letter finally arrived, and when I saw the return address, carrying the letter in from the mailbox, my heart sank. It read:

RACKHAM GRADUATE SCHOOL

Dear Mr. Franklin:

We are pleased to inform you that you have been accepted by the Rackham Graduate School at the University of Michigan and will receive a graduate assistantship in the amount of ...*

Was I accepted because of my prestigious undergraduate school or because of my grade point average or college entrance exam scores— definitely not! More than likely I got in because of the unconventional approach I used, including the passion, politeness, respectful rapport, enthusiasm, determination, and follow-up I demonstrated during what apparently turned out to be an interview. The bottom line? *You cannot optimally showcase your personal and professional demeanor (and passion) in a letter, phone call, or email.* For me, the entire experience, achieving an early breakthrough career goal, via the "magic of a face-to-face meeting," was a "life-changing learning experience."

Orchestrating person-to-person meetings, whenever possible, is a tactic that I've continued to use, with great success, over the past 50 years! I've also learned that in the "real world," people are more likely to hire, do business with, or collaborate with individuals they like and relate to, and those they believe share the same interests and/or values. In-person meetings provide a golden opportunity to convey these traits and build relationships.

Another "Big White Lie": My Trip to the National Library of Medicine, Washington, DC. In 1989, I was nominated by the American Association of Cardiovascular and Pulmonary Rehabilitation Board of Trustees to serve as the next editor-in-chief of the *Journal of Cardiac Rehabilitation* (JCR: 1990–1995)—a prestigious professional appointment that I was honored to accept. Because JCR had been previously declined for inclusion in Index Medicus, meaning that it is listed in the National Library of Medicine (NLM) recommended journal database, that goal became my #1 goal or

---

* During my nearly 6 years of graduate school at the University of Michigan and Penn State University, respectively, my lowest course grade was an A–. ☺

priority. After my most recent application was again denied in January 1994, it was apparent to me that an even more aggressive, unconventional appeals process had to be initiated. But how?

My previous experience, getting into graduate school at the University of Michigan, immediately came to mind, and a "light bulb" went on. I knew what I was going to do. I'd request a face-to-face meeting with the executive editor of Index Medicus at the NLM in Bethesda, Maryland, because I believed it offered a more proactive opportunity to secure the elusive journal designation: *now in Index Medicus*. To reduce the likelihood that my request would be denied, once again, I deceptively told their office that I had frequent meetings in the Washington, DC area, and that I could schedule a meeting with Lois Ann Colaianni, executive director, Index Medicus, on the date and at the time of her choosing. After multiple communications and negotiations with this office, I was offered a very brief period (*only 5 minutes*) to plead the case for the uniqueness and quality of the JCR, and that I'd also receive additional clarification of the requirements necessary to potentially secure JCR's inclusion in Index Medicus.

I prepared a passionate, fact-filled, compelling case for JCR in the 5 minutes I had and essentially practiced, countless times, what I perceived as my closing arguments. When prepping for the challenge, as a Type A personality, I must admit that I studied John Moschitta, Jr., also known as "Motor mouth" John Moschitta and "The Fast Talking Guy," who had the ability to articulate 586 words per minute, and is perhaps best known for his mesmerizing advertisement for FedEx in 1981, titled "Fast Paced World."

When I finished my presentation, there appeared to be an aura of disbelief and amazement in the room, and I'll never forget the smile that erupted on the executive director's face. I flew back to Detroit that evening, knowing that I'd hit a home run and possibly a grand slam. A handwritten thank you note was mailed within a day of my presentation to Ms. Colaianni. In addition, we implemented all of the suggestions that I learned at the meeting that day, including the need for a letter writing campaign to the NLM on the merits of the journal from many of the preeminent scientists and clinicians in the field, along with the fact that the journal had been regularly published for nearly 15 years. Weeks later, I received the following letter from the NLM:

> As you know, the NLM uses an advisory committee, the Literature Selection Review Committee, to review and recommend the journal titles

NLM should index. The Committee recently completed a review of journals for possible inclusion in the NLM's MEDLARS system. I am pleased to inform you that the Journal of Cardiopulmonary Rehabilitation has been selected to be indexed and included in Index Medicus and MEDLINE on the MEDLARS system.

Sincerely yours,
Lois Ann Colaianni,
Executive Director,
Index Medicus.

REJECT REJECTION: TRANSFORMING A "NO" INTO "YES"

According to Jack Canfield and Mark Victor Hansen, rejection doesn't prevent success, but fear of rejection does. And, there is really no good reason to fear rejection (i.e., that your ask will be declined), other than being a bit put-off or embarrassed. Look at it this way—you don't have something—you ask for it—you get a "no"—you're no worse off than when you began. However, as previously discussed, a negative reply or "no" often means "not right now" (for many reasons).

To get what you want, best-selling motivational author Robert Ringer suggests putting the law of averages to work for you with a 10-step approach. Rule #1 is "Ask." Rules 2 through 10 are "Ask again." Ringer contends that the more times you ask for something, the greater the likelihood that you'll ultimately get a "yes"—and one "yes" can cancel out 50"no's." When you get a "no," don't argue. Simply ask why your request was declined. Sometimes, this inquiry alone will change a "no" to a "yes." Then, ask different people, in different ways, at different times. For example, when a service representative says he/she can't help you, thank them, hang up, redial, and speak to another agent. If that representative can't help, ask to speak to a supervisor, and if they can't help, ask them to suggest a higher-level person to call. Finally, ask them if there is anything you can do to help them say "yes" to the request. This casts you as a collaborator, working toward a common goal. Second requests are often accepted, as people don't like to reject two consecutive requests for fear it will make them appear uncooperative, unreasonable, or biased.

In summary, successful people receive the most rejections and "no's" in life. It's a fact! They've learned that it doesn't matter how often you hear "no"—what's important is to *keep acting and asking* until you hear "yes." They've come to realize that if you ask enough times, in varied ways, almost invariably, you'll get what you want.

YOUR FUTURE "ASK PLAN": A PROTOTYPE TO EMULATE

In closing, when asking for something really important to you, whenever possible, set up a face-to-face meeting, even if you have to lie, or "stretch the truth," to obtain access to the key decision maker(s). This pertains, of course, to sales as well. Follow this 11-step plan:

1. Arrange for the face-to-face meeting—at the preferred or convenient time for the decision maker.
2. Before you arrive, do your homework (regarding the decision maker, their company, their mission, recent advancements or innovations, etc.).
3. Arrive at least 15 minutes prior to the scheduled meeting.
4. First impressions count—dress neatly and conservatively, provide a firm handshake to the person you are meeting, maintain eye contact and smile—you are delighted to be there! People form a lasting opinion of you from your handshake—a firm handshake (always in a standing position) suggests you are confident, assertive, and professional.

> You never get a second chance to make a good first impression.
> **Will Rogers**

5. If the opportunity arises, pay the decision maker a professional compliment he/she might be surprised you know—which shows you did your homework, e.g., "I enjoyed reading your recent insightful commentary on population health promotion strategies in the journal of ...."

6. State clearly and concisely why hiring or working with you in a collaborative manner *would be beneficial for them—focus on their needs, not yours.* For them to be sold on you, they've got to like you, feel that you can contribute to their mission, and that you'd be well received by their existing staff. In your discussions, highlight emerging challenges (on the horizon) that may influence their customers, and offer innovative solutions. People generally find your potential more enticing than past accomplishments. If asked about past accomplishments, use this as a springboard to briefly discuss what you can do for them. Listen more than you talk, and allow them to respond. *For job interviews, never ask about benefits, paid days off, or vacation time during the first meeting.* They've got to want you on their team before these issues are discussed.

7. Address their follow-up questions in a "positive" rather than a "put-off" manner.

8. When concluding the meeting, express your sincerest appreciation and gratitude for their time and consideration.

9. Follow up in a timely manner with either a brief email or ideally, a typewritten or handwritten thank you note.

10. Later that day, replay the discussion/interview in your mind. What did you do especially well? What aspects could you improve on? Recognize that these face-to-face meetings are extraordinary learning/training opportunities—make the most of the experience.

11. Finally, think about the original reason or goal that you arranged the face-to-face meeting for, and constantly see it moving toward you. You are going to win some and lose some. What's most important is that your "asks" become more polished and compelling over time—so that the wins far outweigh the losses or setbacks. *Regardless, if you ask more, you'll invariably get more.*

WANT TO DOUBLE YOUR YEARLY SALES AND INCOME?

Double Your Number of Calls

In sales—on commission? Years ago, my son (now a Vice President, Commercial Lending Bank Marketing Manager) mentioned to me how disappointed he was in his yearly sales income—that he had thought it would be twice as high at this point in his career. My suggestion? "Double your monthly 'asks'"! To which he replied, "I'd have to work evenings and weekends." "Yep," I replied. It seemed to get the message across. Today, his annual salary (plus bonuses) is more than 1.5 times my highest ever yearly income—and climbing. And, not surprisingly, he loves his work and takes great pride in the contacts he has cultivated and the successes that he's achieved.

Perhaps the best explanation for this sales approach is the "dart board analogy." Each bullseye represents a sale or success. To hit more bullseyes, you simply need to throw more darts. By throwing more darts, you'll not only get a greater number of chances to hit the bullseye, but your skill will likely increase with more dart throwing (practice), escalating the percentage of successful hits (bullseyes).

9

Be a Communicator: Speaking, Writing, and Interviewing

Perhaps the late Earl Nightingale, author of *Lead the Field* and numerous other success classics, summed it up best: "The higher you climb on a pyramid, the farther you can see, the fresher the air, and the less crowded it becomes. Another rewarding thing about climbing is that as we climb, we help most of those associated with us climb, too." Accordingly, one of the most important ladders leading to the top of any field is KNOWLEDGE. The greater your knowledge, the more power you can exercise over your life and your future. So, where do you start? Begin with proficiency in our language, specifically English, and then progress to your particular area(s) of interest, e.g., sales, business, teaching, medicine, law, etc. Those *two steps*, in that order, can move you over time to the top of the pyramid in your respective field. You'll understand as I proceed.

To an astounding degree, your ability to use our language and the depth and breadth of your vocabulary will determine your income and future success. Broadening your vocabulary increases your mind power and communication skills, making it easier to express your perspectives and viewpoints. Nightingale went on to emphasize that although one may present with stellar academic credentials and a professional, attractive appearance, the moment we open our mouth and begin to speak, people around us take notice. He astutely pointed out that "*our use of our language is the one thing we can't hide.*"

Those who are destined for success invariably become "master communicators" along the way. With practice, they acquire extraordinary speaking/presenting/writing and computer skills. Years ago, *Reader's Digest* published an article by Blake Clark titled, "Words Can Work

DOI: 10.4324/9781003260387-11

Wonders for You." In it, he wrote: "Tests of more than 350,000 persons from all walks of life show that, more often than any other measurable characteristic, knowledge of the exact meanings of a large number of words accompanies outstanding success." Indeed, supporting studies found that:

- A graduating class of a large university was given an English vocabulary examination and followed with surveys during the next 2 decades, asking them about their occupations, annual income, and other markers of success. Without exception, those who scored highest on the vocabulary test were in the top income group, whereas those who scored lowest were in the bottom income group.
- Elementary and high school students with the best vocabularies achieve the highest grades in school.
- In a pioneering study by scientist Johnson O'Connor, vocabulary tests were given to executive and supervisory personnel in 39 large manufacturing plants. Although every one of the staff tested rated high in the aptitudes associated with leadership, vocabulary ratings were highest in presidents and vice presidents, and decreased decrementally among managers, superintendents, foremen, and floor bosses, respectively. In virtually every worker subset, vocabulary correlated with executive/leadership level and annual income.

An added bonus to keep in mind, Blake Clark went on to say,

> is that when we master one word, we find we have added several others. It's as if the new one is a nucleus of thought around which whirl numerous related ideas that we now come to understand. Deliberately learning 10 new words, we pick up probably 90 more, almost without realizing it.

TO EARN MORE, YOU NEED TO LEARN MORE

Leaders are voracious readers—at a minimum, 15 minutes each day, and ideally at least an hour a day. Reading pays off! If you think you don't have time to read, listen to what noted librarian Louis Shores had to say:

> Each of us must find his/her own 15-minute period each day for reading. It's better if it's regular. The only requirement is the will to read. With it, you can find at least 15 minutes, no matter how busy the day.

Shores believed that libraries were places of lifelong learning and that learning should begin early. He extolled the importance of reading to infants and introducing children to books.

The sad reality is that the average American watches 4 or more hours of television each day. I tell my students and junior colleagues to "turn off the damn television and start reading. You're going to get a lot more out of a book than you will from a screen." Moreover, nearly 90 percent of what you see on television today is "negative" information, bombarding the subconscious mind!

When Jack Canfield, co-creator of the blockbuster *Chicken Soup for the Soul®* series, first met his mentor, success guru W. Clement Stone, Stone asked him to eliminate 1 hour of television each day—creating 365 hours per year, corresponding to nine additional 40-hour workweeks or 2 months of additional time each year to accomplish what was most important to him. This recommendation was also echoed by Jim Rohn, America's foremost motivational philosopher, who suggested using that one extra hour a day to read. Early on, Canfield adopted the practice, with specific reference to reading inspirational autobiographies of highly successful people and principles of successful living. He contends that this habit alone, that is, reading at least one book a week, would, over the next 20 years, allow you to read more than 1,000 books, and by applying only a fraction of what you learned from each book, you would be miles ahead of your peers in laying the foundation for an extraordinary life. When Canfield wrote his best-seller *The Success Principles* in 2005, he noted that, at the time, he averaged reading one book every 2 days! Moreover, once you've adopted a regular reading program to improve your proficiency with our language, build on it by adding or complementing it with the specialty area of study, the field(s) that interest you most, by reading everything you can to improve your knowledge, skills, and abilities. This "1-2 approach" should enable you to reach the top 1 percent of experts in your field!

A person who won't read has no advantage over one who can't read.
Mark Twain

Speed Reading + Increased Absorption = Learn More

The best resource I've found to achieve this objective as a self-study course is available through Learning Strategies Corporation (2000

Plymouth Road, Suite 300, Minnetonka, MN 55305-2335; phone: 1-866-292-1861) or online at www.learningstrategies.com.

PRESENTATIONS AND PUBLIC SPEAKING

I love this quote by American writer and broadcaster Lowell Thomas:

> The ability to speak is a short cut to distinction. It puts a man (woman) in the limelight, raises him(her) head and shoulders above the crowd. The individual who can speak acceptably is usually given credit for an ability out of all proportion to what he/she really possesses.

That's true whether you are in front of one person or 3,000 people.

According to Jack Canfield, to speak with impeccability is to speak from your highest self, that is, with intention, integrity, and words that are in alignment with your personal beliefs and actions. When you speak with these underlying principles, your words not only serve to reinforce your vision and perspectives but also have power with others. Canfield further emphasized that to speak with impeccability is to speak only words that are true, that uplift, and that strongly affirm other people's worth. Successful people are conscious of the thoughts they think and the words they speak—both about themselves and about others. "They know that to be more successful, they need to speak words that will build self-esteem and self-confidence, build relationships, and build dreams—words of affirmation, encouragement, appreciation, love, acceptance, possibility, and vision," Canfield added. Unfortunately, this is a far cry from the current political dialogue that we are bombarded with on a daily basis.☹

I remember vividly an undergraduate course I had on public speaking and the response of our remarkable professor when asked to define the characteristics of a superb or notable presentation. Surprisingly, he said:

> It's not so much the information or data that you presented, but how you made the audience feel. Did the talk uplift, motivate, or inspire the listener—evoking a range of emotions—from laughter, to sorrow or concern and perhaps more importantly, did it spur the attendees to take action?

I came to realize that his sentiments captured the essence of the most memorable presentations I had ever heard.

Interestingly, I went to the same professor following class one day—immediately after it was announced that five students, including myself, would be giving their 8-minute talks to the class the following Wednesday. I was absolutely terrified! To potentially delay my speaking debut, I asked the professor if I could give my talk much later in the semester. "Why?" he asked. "Because I'm a horrible presenter and I'm scared to death," I responded. I'll never forget his reply. "Barry, before you are great at something, you've got to be good at it. And, before you are good at it, you've got to be bad. And, before you are bad at it, you've got to try." I did speak on the day that I was assigned, and his experiential sentiments were spot-on. It takes time and *practice, practice, practice* to become a great speaker.

Since those early days, I've heard countless mediocre-to-average speakers and many good-to-great presenters. I've also given well over 1,000 invited presentations myself, locally, nationally, and internationally, and have been coached by media and speaker consultants. To be frank with you, I rarely get nervous anymore, even "with live television interviews." The secret? Simply blot out camera crews and video equipment, SMILE, enthusiastically talk directly to the media person who is interviewing you—and have a couple of relevant canned talking points, regardless of the questions posed. What did I learn about presenting? I learned a lot!

You can markedly improve your presentation skills by carefully observing the styles of extraordinary speakers, emulating aspects of those who are *passionate about their topic* and exhibit organizational wizardry, contagious enthusiasm, voice modulations, eye contact, and humor—ideally, self-deprecating humor. Second, find a fabulous speaker who can serve as your mentor. Third, practice, practice, practice—willingly accept all invitations, and even work behind the scenes to obtain them, because repeated practice unequivocally improves presentation performance. (Malcolm Gladwell [*Outliers*] reminds us of the 10,000-hour rule — you really don't get great at something until you've devoted 10,000+ hours to the skill or craft.) Finally, devour some of the best books on public speaking, including two of my favorites: *I Can See You Naked: A Fearless Guide to Making Great Presentations* by Ron Hoff; and *Speak with Confidence: Powerful Presentations That Inform, Inspire, and Persuade* by Dianna Booher.

What else did I learn about great presentations? Captivating speakers pause briefly before speaking; they stand silent. Every second you wait before speaking, you grow in stature. *In addition, the first 90 seconds of any presentation are crucial.* Oftentimes, up to 54 percent of the audience have already tuned you out within this time frame. What are they thinking about? The most common distractors?

Distractors: What Is the Audience Thinking About?

Topic	%
Business/work concerns	39
Family/health problems	33
Upcoming travel	25
Recreational engagement	19
Conflict with boss/co-worker	12
Room temperature	8
Interpersonal relations/sexual fantasies*	6

* Primarily men

To avoid losing your audience in the first 90 seconds, speakers must *open dramatically* with an attention grabber to capture their audience. Although we could provide countless examples, perhaps few opening lines are more famous than President Franklin Delano Roosevelt's Pearl Harbor address:

> Mr. Vice President, Mr. Speaker, Members of the Senate, and of the House of Representatives:
> Yesterday, December 7th, 1941—a date which will live in infamy—the United States of America was suddenly and deliberately attacked by naval and air forces of the Empire of Japan.
> The United States was at peace with that nation and, at the solicitation of Japan, was still in conversation with its government and its emperor looking toward the maintenance of peace in the Pacific ....
> I ask that the Congress declare that since the unprovoked and dastardly attack by Japan on Sunday, December 7th, 1941, a state of war has existed between the United States and the Japanese empire.

As for me, I try to build a "people connection" within the first minute of any presentation by getting the audience to smile or, ideally, laugh out loud. Accordingly, I'll often personalize the presentation to the audience or local area by telling them, up front, that I'm always very nervous before I give a "big talk" (like this one) and that I'm also a highly superstitious person. As a result, I've gotten into the habit of buying a copy of the local newspaper, their newspaper, that day, and reading my horoscope before the "big talk." I personalize it by always complimenting the audience in the horoscope and make it local by finding out and citing the name of the most widely read newspaper in the area. In fact, this is generally my first question to the hotel registration staff after landing in a new city where I will be speaking.

For example, I gave a Saturday evening presentation before a large medical audience in the Lake Tahoe, California, area, opened up with the first slide showing my horoscope that day (I'm a Gemini), and highlighted the accuracy and irony of my forecast.

HOROSCOPE:

Gemini (May 21 – June 21)
   Today will be a banner day for you. You'll give a GREAT after dinner presentation before an attractive, intelligent, highly accomplished, medically oriented audience. Deafening applause and/or standing ovation are likely.

November 9, 2019
Reno Gazette Journal

The horoscope actually changes little from city to city, with slight modifications made for the audience I'm speaking to (e.g., physicians, business-industry, nurses, general public), the local newspaper, and the specific date I'm speaking. It's always followed by big smiles and boisterous laughter and, at the conclusion of many talks, gets me a standing ovation, especially when I show the last slide, which reveals a well-dressed audience standing and applauding, with one person saying to another, "great talk."☺

WHAT ARE THE KEYS TO A CAPTIVATING POWERPOINT PRESENTATION?

- *Features:* If possible, include eye-catching pictures, animation, and graphics; the background and font colors should be compatible, distinctive, and soothing on the eyes (dark blue, yellows, and whites are preferred colors); and the font should be readable in size—avoid putting too much on one slide. In addition, avoid having too much empty space on the slide; fill it up with text and pictures. On the first slide, in addition to the title of your presentation, include your name, degree, and email address, and acknowledge your business or institution's name and/or logo.

- *Tell the audience, up front, the precise goal or message you intend to convey and the number of topics you plan to cover in the specific designated time frame.* Great presentations are characterized by clarity, conveying fewer messages but backed by authoritative research-based facts and memorable examples. A "build slide" can be helpful in this regard; it starts with the first bullet point highlighted, with the others dim, and as the presentation proceeds, the new topic is highlighted, and the previous and upcoming topics are dimmed. As a general rule, most 50- to 60-minute talks cover three to eight topics. Many educational, scientific, clinical, and business presentations are 10 to 30 minutes in duration and cover decrementally fewer topics.

Build Slides

Outline	→	• Physical	→	• Physical	→	• Physical
• **Physical Activity**		Activity		Activity		Activity
• Fitness		• **Fitness**		• Fitness		• Fitness
• Health Implications		• Health Implications		• **Health Implications**		• Health Implications
• Conclusions		• Conclusions		• Conclusions		• **Conclusions**

Depending on the length of your presentation, and how much time you spend on each topic, there might be 2 to 20 slides after each "build slide." Transitions move one slide off the screen and the next one on, and the format and speed of each transition can be varied.

- *Use the word "you" often; maintain eye contact with your audience; smile (it increases your likeability); and, if possible, positively or favorably mention people's names in the audience when they relate to the topic you are discussing.*
- *Use REPETITION to emphasize key points to the audience.* Your audience is more likely to remember something that has been

repeated during your talk. I'll often make an important point during a talk and restate it in my closing slide(s) titled, "Take Home Messages." Repetition is powerful because it can make a message more persuasive, more memorable, and more believable.

Sidebar. And, while we are talking about the impact that repetition has on making your talking points even more believable, I want to call your attention to the powerful effect of repetition or reiteration on the human mind—in changing people's behaviors and getting what you want in life. Perhaps Claude Bristol summed it up best when he referred to the "tap, tap, tap, tap" of the pneumatic chisel, with a terrific force behind it causing the disintegration of particles that makes the holes in solid concrete or steel into which it is placed. On the other hand, you may not appreciate the profound impact that repeated repetition has on people, including yourself. The fundamental of advertising is its repetition, its appeal by reiteration—"Safe drivers save 40 percent" (Allstate Insurance); "Liberty Mutual—only pay for what you need"; Maxwell House coffee, "Good to the last drop"; and Coca-Cola, "The pause that refreshes." Indeed, many of the often-repeated advertising phrases in commercials become part of our language. I've also seen skilled prosecutors and clever defenders subtly appeal to the emotions of jurors by repeating and emphasizing time after time the points they wish to stress. Behind all the talk is that tap, tap, tap, tap—tapping the subconscious—making the jurors believe their contentions. "If the glove doesn't fit, you must acquit" was constantly repeated during the trial of O.J. Simpson. During the great depression, smart politicians kept emphasizing "Business is coming back"—repetition, reiteration—again and again. Tap, tap, tap.

I wish I had a dollar for every time I heard President Trump reiterate, "No obstruction, no collusion!" and additional Trump "tap, tap, taps" such as "Sleepy Joe," "best economy ever," and "there is nobody who has done more for ...." More recently, his oft-repeated election comments included: "The election had been stolen"; "If you count the legal votes, I easily win"; "What they are doing is a hoax with the ballot"; and "This is going to be a fraud election like you've never seen." If people hear something often enough, particularly when it's fueled by some 24/7 media outlets, regardless of whether it is true or false, they begin to believe it.

Bristol further emphasized that if you can get a detailed picture in your subconscious mind of something that you want, and use the process of reiteration and repetition to keep the picture(s) before you constantly every day, in every way, you'll have at your command a power that astounds. To this end, he emphasizes that the world's most successful men and women live daily with their goals "in mind." This tap, tap, tap approach, visualizing what they want over and over, provides a gravitational positional system (GPS) to move them in the right direction, strangely attracting the resources, collaborators, and opportunities they need to bring their objectives to fruition. Miracles will occur—and you will do what you may have previously thought was impossible.

- *The magic number?* The *rule of three* in public speaking. The rule is a very general principle stating that ideas presented in *threes* are inherently more interesting, more enjoyable, and more memorable for your audience. Commercials have relied on this rule for many years. "Where's the beef?" "Coke is it." "Just do it."

Some very famous speeches have also embraced the *rule of three*. Barak Obama's inaugural speech:

Homes have been lost; jobs shed; businesses shuttered.

Abraham Lincoln's Gettysburg Address:

But, in a larger sense, we cannot dedicate, we cannot consecrate, we cannot hallow this ground .... —and that government of the people, by the people, for the people, shall not perish from the earth.

- *Use alliteration when presenting (or writing) to highlight important phrases with the repetition of sounds.* When using alliteration, words that begin with the same sound are placed close together (e.g., the subtitle of this book). It makes the phrase easy to memorize and fun to read or say out loud.

His record reflects performance, not promises.

Many great speakers have used alliteration to emphasize certain aspects of their arguments or perspectives. Consider Martin Luther King Jr.'s famous quote:

I have a dream that my four children will one day live in a nation where they will not be judged by the color of their skin but by the content of their character.

Alliteration is also widely used in advertising and business names for easy memorization, in the naming of celebrities and cartoon characters, and in media slogans.

Examples of Alliteration

Business	Naming	Media Slogans
• American Airlines	• Donald Duck	• "What gift should … you give your guy?"
• Best Buy	• Mickey Mouse	
• Coca-Cola	• Porky Pig	
• Dunkin Donuts	• Marilyn Monroe	• "The lives they lived."
• Krispy Kreme	• Sammy Sosa	

- *The delivery*: Use voice modulations, changing your tone and pitch, to reflect confidence and instill passion and emotion in the ideas and beliefs you are attempting to convey. Never try to memorize your talk or read it from a script. You'll immediately lose credibility, alienate your listeners, and dampen audience attention! Avoid speaking in a monotone, and put emphasis on certain words. Indeed, voice modulation is one of the most powerful tools that you can have in your arsenal while delivering a presentation. Speak slowly and authoritatively, and *practice, practice, practice* before giving the talk, with specific reference to timing your delivery to introduce, clarify, and highlight the supporting slides that you may be simultaneously presenting. Look at your audience. A technique used by many captivating speakers is to catch the eye of one audience member at a time and pretend you're briefly speaking to him/her only—then move on to another.
- Recognize that the most entertaining, informative, and captivating speakers are *storytellers* who can elicit a range of emotions. Be entertaining, and make the audience smile, laugh, or cry. I'll never forget my undergraduate speech teacher who first shared this secret with me. He said: "It's not so much what you say in a talk, but how you made the audience feel. Great speakers use well-timed

quotations, ask rhetorical questions, and share funny, motivational and inspirational stories to make the point."

Sidebar. As an example, Joseph C. Piscatella, a good friend and an esteemed colleague (we've written two books together), is, in my humble opinion, one of *the very best speakers in the country* on how to live a healthy lifestyle. At the age of 32, he underwent triple vessel heart bypass surgery, and now in his mid-70s, he's got some memorable practical perspectives that audiences value. Joe is truly a master at using stories and anecdotes to make a point. Audiences smile and laugh out loud throughout his presentations.

One of my all-time favorite Piscatella stories was when Joe got two speeding tickets in a 20-minute period—substantiating his Type A personality. His wife Bernie had requested he drive his children and some visiting children from Germany down the breathtaking Oregon coastline, but in a limited time frame. Joe's heavy foot unfortunately led to a speeding ticket—which caused him to lose some valuable time! So, what did Joe do? After being stopped and getting the speeding ticket, he found himself gradually increasing his driving speed to make up for the lost time, looked in his rearview mirror, and saw a flashing "red light" with another police car pulling him over to stop. When the officer approached the car full of kids, requesting his driver's license, he asked Joe "how long has it been since your last ticket?" One of Joe's children replied, "not that long ago." Joe adeptly uses the art of storytelling, contagious humor, and memorable experiences to empower audiences to remember the health-related information and advice that he shares.

- *Build a people connection* (e.g., why is the information you are presenting of interest to them?) and personalize the presentation to the area, audience, or news of the day. However, be sensitive to potential topical areas that may be irritating, disparaging, prejudiced, or repugnant to your audience. Proactively identify topics/phrases that could be offensive or negatively perceived, and avoid them—like age, gender, politics, working class, education, religion, body habitus, and colloquialisms. If you use humorous anecdotes throughout the talk, make yourself the one to poke fun at. When possible, slip in praise for your audience into the middle of your talk, since people generally respond in kind.

- *Dress for power or authority.* Men: gray or navy suits with white or blue shirts and red tie; women: tailored suits in solid colors.
- *Stay on time, close with a flourish, and briefly restate key messages.* Audience surveys reveal: "Up to 70 percent of all presentations are too long." *Learn to stay on time or end a few minutes early.* Don't just unimaginatively state your closing remarks—make them memorable by slightly raising your voice, or make theatre of them. Closing with a powerful story or summary is the best way to get a standing ovation. When concluding a presentation, I'll often show a WOW slide— multi-colored, animation, eye-catching funny pictures with three closing take home messages. The *rule of three* plays magnificently at the end of any presentation—and can bring the audience to its feet (especially if you preface your talk with today's horoscope slide that I alluded to earlier). Alternatively, pull out a small piece of paper or note card and put on reading glasses to make people anticipate what you are about to tell them. Finally, motivate the audience to take action.
- *Welcome questions!* Each comment or question is an indicator of interest and allows you the opportunity to clarify individual misinterpretations of the information you presented. In many cases, a speaker who can adeptly answer questions during the Q/A period, can substantively enhance the audience's overall rating of his/her presentation. As a general rule, I try to avoid confrontations or arguments during these interchanges, and oftentimes respond to audience members' comments with "I could not agree with you more." But …. *pause briefly before answering, which conveys respect, thought, and a careful measured response to their query.*

PRESENTATION TIP: HANDLING QUESTIONS DURING AND AFTER YOUR TALK

During a slide show, someone will sometimes ask a question that's unrelated to the slide onscreen. When this happens, you want to focus attention on the question at hand, not on the slide. Or, you might be ready to give the audience a break, but you didn't plant a signal slide in your presentation. In these situations, all you need to do is display a black (or white) screen. Doing so gives the impression that you've pulled up a blank slide for the occasion.

Fortunately, you can blank the screen during a slide show with one simple keystroke. To display a black screen, press the B key. If you'd rather display a white screen, simply press the W key. When you press the B or W key a second time, the slide show picks up where you left off: The slide displayed when you blanked the screen appears again.

P.S. Don't be afraid or embarrassed to say "I don't know" to a specific question. Why? There's a subdued power in confidently stating that you don't know something. Believe it or not, it actually gives you additional credibility as a speaker.

IMPROVE YOUR WRITING SKILLS

THE POWER OF WORDS: A SIGN CHANGE THAT OPENED PEOPLE'S EYES AND THEIR WALLETS

An old beggar sat on a busy street corner, next to a metal pail, asking for spare change from passersby. His hand-held sign read: "I'm blind, please help." Most people walked briskly past the man. A young woman noticed this and asked if she could change his sign. Not knowing what she had written, he soon felt like he had hit the jackpot, as coins increasingly filled his pail. Later, on her way to lunch, the lady stopped by to see him. He asked, "how did you change my sign?" "I simply scrawled some words that made people realize something they took for granted," she replied. "It's a beautiful day, and I can't see."

One of the best ways to improve your writing (and speaking) skills is to learn from veteran role models and highly skilled mentors. Ralph Waldo Emerson wrote, "Hitch your wagon to a star." Virtually every accomplished writer I know will tell me, "I studied with so-and-so .... I worked with so-and-so .... it was the best learning experience I ever had .... he was the master .... she was the master. I learned so much from them. He/she taught me how to write."

As a graduate student, whose responsibilities included teaching and writing a master's and PhD thesis, respectively, early on, I took a heightened interest in my presentation (public speaking) and writing skills. Although continued graduate school training and education, no doubt, helped to enhance these skills, it became glaringly apparent to me that I needed additional help in improving these critically important communication proficiencies. Accordingly, I sought to work with (i.e., hitch my wagon to) accomplished writers, editors, and highly prolific scientists, researchers, and clinicians to improve these skills.

Professor Elsworth R. Buskirk, a physiologist par excellence and my PhD advisor at Penn State University, was one of my first mentors in this regard. I vividly recall meeting with him one day to discuss the initial draft of my PhD thesis. "I finished reading your dissertation draft. On page 92, what do you mean when you state, maximal oxygen consumption or VO_2max changed appreciably in a positive manner or direction, over the course of the physical conditioning program?" he asked. "It increased," I replied. "Uh, huh. Well, then just say post-conditioning VO_2max increased significantly," Buskirk responded. He was truly a man of few words. He went on to teach me an indelible lesson ..."there, I've just said in four words what you stated in twenty-one! When writing from a clinical or scientific perspective, each word costs you \$1. Accordingly, I've just saved you \$17. When it comes to scientific writing, brevity and conciseness are virtues," he added.

Subsequently, I went to work as an assistant professor with my most demanding mentor, Herman K. Hellerstein, MD, a world-renowned cardiologist whose curriculum vitae, from all of his pioneering research publications, was the largest I had ever seen! We wrote many scientific reports and book chapters together—and by noting his infinite edits and amplifications on my work, my writing skills further improved. Indeed, one of the highlights of my early career was co-authoring with him a particular chapter that he had been asked to write. After countless frustrating revisions and re-revisions at his request, I made all my suggested final changes to both his sections and mine and gave it back to him (my heart in my mouth) for his final review. It was sent to the publisher with only one additional modification: The order of the authors had been changed, by him, from "Hellerstein and Franklin" to "Franklin and Hellerstein." How did I feel? My grueling and self-deprecating experience could perhaps best be described by two classic hits: "Eye of the Tiger" by Survivor, and "Don't Stop Believing" by Journey.

Without question, however, the best career decision I ever made was moving from Sinai Hospital (Detroit) to William Beaumont Hospital (Royal Oak, MI), where I had the opportunity to work with the co-director of cardiology, Gerald C. Timmis, MD, a nationally known clinical and interventional cardiologist, editor, researcher, and writer who, every year, published a book providing an update on the world's cardiology literature, titled *Cardiovascular Review*. In addition to a generous salary increase, Dr. Timmis offered me the prospect to serve as one of several co-authors on his widely acclaimed annual text—an opportunity I simply could not turn down. His superb administrative assistant, Brenda White, who orchestrated the book each year, gave each of the co-authors a huge stack (several hundred) of recent reprints every spring, which purportedly were organized on the Timmis pool table, to succinctly summarize each individual report via dictation in varied categories and to have everything back to her and Dr. Timmis by early fall. I joked to family, friends, and colleagues—it was a great way to have your summer fly by! Although I thought I was a pretty good writer going into this annual herculean endeavor, I was initially horrified and pissed off by the extensive Timmis handwritten edits and snide (and sometimes X-rated comments) that covered my sections. But I quickly came to the sobering realization that I wasn't as good a writer as I thought I was. Working closely with "the master," Dr. Gerald Timmis, over the years took my writing skills to far greater heights—a priceless experience!

Over the past two decades, I've further refined these skills by writing/ editing numerous additional books (this one is my 27th), research reports, chapters, manuscript reviews, editing our *State of the Heart* patient newsletter, and mentoring countless students, residents, cardiology fellows, and younger colleagues around the world by helping them with their publications. The latter has also served to quadruple my productivity and publications. Indeed, the dividends of collaboration are mindboggling and provide regular opportunities for practice, practice, practice. There is no mystery about this cause and effect relation, it's just so. I've now personally tallied ~35,000 to 40,000 hours of writing/editing and am invariably adding to this total. In fact, a student recently asked me how often each week I'm involved in writing and/or editing manuscripts, articles, and other documents. "Only on the days that I eat," I replied.

ADVERTISING A PRODUCT OR SERVICE? WORDS MATTER

A locksmith in Portland, Oregon had a sign in his shop that read, "Keys made while you wait." It occurred to him that people don't like to wait. So he changed the sign to read: "Keys made while you watch." Within a year, his business doubled!

Moral of the story? What we write (or say) has a lot to do with whether people listen to us. How we say it (the words we use) has everything to do with whether they hear us.

Other strategies to improve your writing skills include:

- Overcome writer's block. (The late Louis L'Amour, one of the best-selling authors of all time, when asked the key to his writing style, responded: "Start writing, no matter what. The water doesn't flow until the faucet is turned on.")
- Use the opening paragraph to set the stage/rationale.
- Write first drafts (sections) freely and quickly.
- Write persuasively with a "you" attitude. Put the reader in the message.
- Support your writing arguments with evidence that is credible (i.e., research-based).
- Review first and subsequent drafts to eliminate unnecessary words and to improve the clarity and readability of the document (*Note*: Whenever I submit a manuscript to an editor or publisher, they are being sent a draft that has already been revised multiple times. Although some may believe it's a first draft, and that I'm a brilliant writer, in my experience, well-written documents are invariably the result of countless revisions.)
- Become an active member and ultimately a "fellow" of a professional organization(s) related to your field—which offers writing opportunities for association newsletters, journals, books, white papers, research abstracts, editorials, and commentaries.
- Get a skilled mentor to review/edit your work.
- PRACTICE, PRACTICE, PRACTICE!

TOP 10 REASONS TO DEVELOP EXTRAORDINARY SPEAKING AND WRITING SKILLS

#10	Speaking and writing will empower you to read and learn more, which confers a greater likelihood of noteworthy professional success.
# 9	Knowledge is one of the most important ladders leading to the top of any field. The greater your knowledge, the more power you can exercise over your life and future.
# 8	Studies have shown that your ability to use our language and the depth and breadth of your vocabulary will largely determine your income ceiling and future success.
# 7	Broadening and expanding your vocabulary increases your mind power and communication skills, making it easier to articulately express your perspectives and viewpoints.
# 6	Investigations of people from all walks of life reveal that, more than any other characteristic, knowledge of the exact meanings of a large number of words accompanies outstanding success.
# 5	People who develop extraordinary speaking and/or writing skills often gravitate to leadership positions. These skills, especially the former, provide a short cut to distinction, raising them head and shoulders above their peers.
# 4	Speaking and writing are both forms of sowing—you'll reap the rewards, which, invariably, will exceed your expectations.
# 3	Like so many life skills, speaking and writing are enhanced by great mentoring and practice. Practice, practice, practice—willingly accept invitations, and even work behind the scenes to obtain them, because repeated practice unequivocally improves performance.
# 2	I've learned that you never know who may be reading your writing or in the audience during a presentation you give. The added visibility will yield unexpected opportunities that you never imagined, leading to more visibility and more opportunities.
# 1	Regardless of your field, outstanding speaking and writing skills will provide you with a gateway to success … talents and training that will keep on giving (indefinitely).

INTERVIEWING: PRACTICE PEARLS

Finding a job can be challenging, especially when you are "unproven" and in the early stages of your career. To find a job, consider using LinkedIn .com and Twitter. Recommendations to jumpstart a stalled job search and increase the likelihood of successful interviewing and landing a job include:

- *Your cover letter.* Don't email your cover letter—mail it. Your typewritten communication should focus on the prospective employer and their needs. For example, say something like, "You will benefit from my graduate training, professional certifications, and 6 years of experience in helping patients like yours in research-based health promotion interventions." Or, alternatively, "I believe my previous training and work experience can help companies like yours in growing their staff, sales, and market share." When possible, briefly describe a previous work-related challenge you faced and how you approached and resolved it. Alternatively, highlight new information relevant to their company's mission. Always end the letter with a P.S. (readers' eyes automatically go to the P.S.). "P.S. I'd appreciate the opportunity to meet with you to discuss how my training and experience can help advance your department's formidable mission and strategic plan."

- *Prepare for the interview.* Upload your most flattering head shot on to your LinkedIn.com or social media pages. A photo tells prospective employers that you want to be found and puts you at the top of their contact lists. Also, recognize that modern-day job interviews are far less focused on past accomplishments. A recent study from Waggl, a real-time listening platform, revealed that 85 percent of business and human resources directors believe that interview responses are more insightful than a resume in identifying future talent and cultural fit. The table at the conclusion of this section lists many of the most common questions posed to those interviewing for positions, and a few unconventional ones. These should be carefully reviewed by potential job candidates, and individual, experience-based positive responses should be prepared ahead of time—and even rehearsed by working with a friend or family member. By reviewing these questions, or variations of them, you can largely prevent being blindsided by your interviewer.

- *Phone or Zoom interview first? Prepare.* If the company first requests a phone or Zoom interview before inviting you in for a face-to-face interview, be prepared, upbeat, enthusiastic, and polite. If given a choice between placing the interview phone call and receiving it, opt to receive, and take the call on a landline. Dress professionally for it. Take a lozenge or a teaspoon of honey one hour before the interview (place a cup of water near the phone). Eliminate background noise (e.g., a barking dog). Answer the phone with a smile within two rings and maintain the smile throughout the interview. Say "hello," not "hi," and avoid "ums," and "you knows." Although you may not realize it, a smile makes the tone of your voice more appealing, and approximately 70 percent of how you're perceived on the phone is based solely on the tone of your voice. Make your responses to all queries/comments, including small talk (e.g., weather), relatively concise (e.g., 30 to 90 seconds). An additional advantage you have with a phone interview is that you can (*and should*) have some handwritten notes in front of you as reminders to emphasize some key points about the company and your qualifications. Promptly follow up the phone interview with an email and/or professional note to the interviewer, emphasizing how you can help their company.

- *Research the company and your interviewer, if possible, before your face-to-face interview.* Arrive early (at least 15 minutes) and bring with you a copy of your updated resume and list of references. Employers generally rely on references to confirm that potential employees have good people skills and a strong work ethic. Put together two or three powerful references before your interview and have them in hand to give to the interviewer. Avoid using family and friends as references. Always ask a former professor, manager, director, supervisor, or co-worker for permission to use their name before listing them. Along with your resume, your reference sheet should include your name, address, and contact information, along with a listing of each reference and their complete information (name, job title, employer, address [city, state, zip code], phone number, and email address). You should also provide information regarding their relation to you and how long you have known them.

OVERUSED CAREER BUZZWORDS TO DELETE
IN YOUR RESUME/COVER LETTER

- responsible
- strategic
- expert
- organizational

- creative
- effective
- patient

- driven
- innovative
- analytical

(Sources: CareerBliss.com and FoxBusiness.com)

- *Interviewing 101: The basics.* When interviewing face-to-face, arrive well-groomed, with fresh breath, and professionally dressed (conservative business suit or sport coat), and greet the interviewer with a slow-flooding smile (let your smile build) and by simultaneously introducing yourself (e.g., "Good morning, I'm Jennifer Garner") with a firm handshake, while looking directly at them. If given the interviewer's business card, treat it with respect. Pause to read it and carefully place it in a briefcase or purse. During your meeting, maintain eye contact with the interviewer, smile, share personal stories, and if possible, mention something positive about the company and/or the interviewer that he/she might be surprised you know—demonstrating that you did your homework. For example: "I agree with your sentiments, Mr. Smith, regarding future directions in telecommunications, as I read your recent excellent commentary on that topic published in *Business Weekly*."
- *Related interviewing etiquette.* Stride into the room with confidence, and remove hands/thumbs from your pockets. Respect the interviewer's personal space by noting how far from you they feel comfortable interacting. Focus on the interviewer's face. Don't stare, but make strong eye contact. Recognize that 60 to 80 percent of all communication is nonverbal and that body language during the interview matters. Avoid too frequent or too enthusiastic nodding. Maintain an upright rather than slouched posture during the interview, sit forward in your chair, chin up, both feet on the floor, and don't cross legs or arms (suggests defensiveness) or repeatedly touch your face or hair (interpreted as dishonesty). Hand steepling, touching the fingertips together with the hands pointed up and fingers spread wide (i.e., in a prayer-like gesture), signals confidence in your thoughts and dedication to your point of view. Also, to avoid wasting time during your interview, know exactly where key materials (e.g., resume, letters of reference) are in your briefcase.

Finally, leave your phone and electronics off or on silent mode and out of sight.

- Think/talk in terms of their interests, rather than yours, and generally keep your responses to their questions between 30 and 90 seconds (maximum).

- *Demonstrate "good people skills" during the interview.* Say "please," "thank you," and "you're welcome" rather than "sure," "yep," or "no problem." Ever wonder why you have two ears and one mouth? It's so you listen more and say less. Pay attention to the interviewer— listening is an essential people skill that builds trust, displays sincerity, and shows you value the input of others. Indeed, the famous Austrian pianist, poet, artist, and author Alfred Brendel noted that the word "listen" contains the same letters as "silent." The person being interviewed should not respond before the interviewer is finished talking. As a general guideline, one should pause two to three seconds before answering any interviewer's question—as it conveys respect, thought, and a measured response.

- *Likeability counts!* Make the interviewer like you, and a job offer is more likely on the horizon. Stay positive in everything you say. Listen attentively, don't be afraid to say "I don't know," and if you can't say something complimentary or nice, say nothing. Look for words or clues to help build rapport (e.g., love of dogs, hobbies, areas of interest). *The best way to bond with the interviewer is to discover common interests.* Most people will act toward you as you act toward them; thus, remember: Smiles and enthusiasm are contagious. Another essential ingredient of a good personality is a sense of humor. Learn to laugh more at yourself and at the situations that life presents. When queried, preface some responses with "I believe," or "I may be wrong about this, but ...," which suggests you would certainly consider alternative viewpoints. Use the same terms as your interviewer. This increases the likelihood that he/she will feel comfortable with you. Be prepared to handle small talk; tell brief (30–90 seconds), enlightening stories about yourself. Good signs are if you can get the interviewer to laugh or smile, or if the interview lasts a lot longer than you anticipated.

  Researchers at Harvard and Duke examined the importance of like-ability in the business world. What did they find? "When faced with a choice between a 'competent jerk' and a 'lovable fool' as a work partner, people (and that includes interviewers) usually opt for likeability over ability." Interestingly, over competency, education, and experience, the best colleagues share one simple quality—they are likeable.

Remember, you are there to sell the interviewer on YOU! Are you the kind of person that they (and their colleagues) would like to see and work with on a daily basis? Executives will also tell you their #1 priority in new hires is "the ability to work with people." Exude "good people skills" and a positive demeanor during the interview. Make the interviewer think you'd be a pleasant person to have around. Avoid controversy (politics, religion, personal topics) and making any negative comments on your current or former boss or employer, or the university you graduated from. Refrain from talking non-stop about your favorite subject—YOU. In addition, cultivate an aura of humility and being soft spoken, as opposed to "the party doesn't start till I walk in!" Finally, being well-read and informed about the world around you empowers you to respond to any question that may come your way.

- *Common interview mistakes.* There are four major mistakes that job interviewers often cite as reasons why applicants were not selected. These include: failing to explain their previous work responsibilities; showing off or bragging during the interview; inadequately answering the questions that were posed; and, acting like a robot—showing little or no enthusiasm or passion. Avoid these common pitfalls!
- *Concluding the interview.* If the interviewer asks you if you have any questions, ask about the job, its responsibilities, and unique opportunities for professional growth. Avoid questions regarding pay, personal days off, paid holidays, sick days, health benefits, and vacation time until it appears a job offer will be forthcoming. As you are preparing to leave, it's fine to ask the interviewer about next steps or when you might expect to hear from them. Close the interview with a firm handshake and a sincere thank you to the interviewer for his/her time and consideration.

GOOD QUESTIONS TO ASK AT THE END OF A JOB INTERVIEW

1. What type of personalities do well here?
2. What personal and professional opportunities does the company offer?

3. What is the typical career path for people in the position I'm applying for?
4. What is the company culture like?
5. Why do you like working here?
6. What values are important to the company?

* *After the interview.* Suggest you email a thank you note to the interviewer on the day of the interview, and mail a typed, formal thank you letter to the interviewer the same day as well. Don't delay! This is a BIG DEAL—and could make the difference in what gets you the job (i.e., all other factors equal, this candidate [YOU] went a little bit further to confirm their desire to work at a given place by sending this letter).

    Sidebar. Years ago, we posted a full-time nursing position in our department and received 10 qualified applicants for it. We narrowed it down to the final three. One of the three mailed a thank you note to me, the department director, and to our manager.

    Mine read:

Dear Doctor Franklin:

"Thank you so very much for the opportunity to interview for your nursing position at Beaumont Hospital.

I was so impressed by the work you are doing and the wonderful staff that I met. Would love to be part of your team!

If selected for the position, I promise — you won't be disappointed."

Sincerely, A.D.

We hired her! Why? Because she went a bit further than all the other candidates. And, it's true, she didn't disappoint — and far exceeded our high expectations. An extraordinary nurse who is still with us after more than two decades. Her actions *after* the interview highlight an important principle in achieving our goals: Success doesn't happen by chance.

JOB REJECTION? SMART NEXT STEPS

Because most jobs today have two or more final candidates, the likelihood is that you may not be selected. If you are notified that you were not chosen for the position, send a thank you note for letting you know, expressing your disappointment, and reiterating your continued interest in working there. Include your contact information. Why? Sometimes the newly hired person does not work out, or ends up accepting another position that they simultaneously applied for. Perhaps baseball legend Yogi Berra summed it up best when he said: "It ain't over till it's over."

"TOP 32" COMMON (AND UNCONVENTIONAL) JOB INTERVIEW QUESTIONS (BE PREPARED)

1. "Tell me about yourself."
2. "Why do you want to work here?"
3. "Tell me about a pivotal leadership experience in your career. What did you learn and how do you apply that today?"
4. "What was your undergraduate grade point average, and do you believe it provides an indicator of your potential performance in working for our company? If not, why?"
5. "How do you approach someone who is not cooperative?"
6. "How would your current or former co-workers describe you?"
7. "What is an example of constructive feedback that you regularly receive? What have you done to improve on that?"
8. "Who is your hero and why?"
9. "Tell me about a time when you received negative feedback from a customer, client, supervisor, or patient. How did you address this feedback, and what was the final outcome?"
10. "Tell me about a time when you made a decision in the workplace that turned out to be a mistake."
11. "Have you ever been in a position where you disagreed with a supervisor's decision or directive? What did you do?"
12. "Tell me how you've approached change in the work environment."

13. "What are you really into outside of work (e.g., hobbies, recreation, volunteering, family)?"
14. "How do you learn best, and keep up with recent advances in the field?"
15. "How many messages are in your inbox right now?" "How do you manage email?"
16. "What's the last book you read for business or pleasure and how long ago did you finish it?" "What journals do you regularly read or review to stay up on the field?"
17. "Are you a member of any professional organizations or associations? If so, why, if not, why not?"
18. "On a scale of 1 (very low) to 10 (very high), how lucky are you?"
19. "In one word, describe yourself."
20. "Assuming there is only one job (leaving aside our position opening for now) that you could apply for at this stage of your career, where would you apply and why?"
21. "In the next 2 minutes, teach me something related to your field (area of expertise) that I do not know."
22. "What do you often think about when you are completely alone?"
23. "Tell me about a time when you went 'above and beyond' in attempting to satisfy a customer or client."
24. "What would you do to improve the productivity, efficiency, and overall job satisfaction of staff who are working under your direction?"
25. "When it's all over, how do you want to be remembered?"

UNCONVENTIONAL JOB INTERVIEW QUESTIONS—BE PREPARED!

26. "How lucky are you, and why?" (Upbeat, positive people tend to consider themselves lucky and realize that, to a large extent, we make our own luck.)
27. "How would you rate (1, poor; 10, excellent) me as an interviewer?" (Obviously, you don't want to belittle or disparage the interviewer, but responding with a "10" makes you look like someone who may evade difficult conversations or be unwilling to provide constructive feedback.

To evoke a smile, I'd probably respond a strong "7" to "8"; however, if I'm offered the position, it would probably increase to "9" to "10.") ☺

28. "Describe the color 'yellow' to someone who is blind." (If the person has always been blind, describe "yellow" using senses other than sight. A good answer might be, "yellow is warm, like the sun on your skin on a pleasant summer day.")

29. "Who would win a fight between Spiderman and Batman?" Assume each has their usual armamentarium and the battleground is neutral. (Pick one and defend your answer with whatever knowledge you have on these superheroes. Failing to pick one would make you appear indecisive.)

30. "If you were a Muppet, which Muppet would you be?" (A good answer might be Yoda, the Muppet created for the Star Wars movies. Yoda was intelligent, patient, thoughtful, and willing to share his knowledge.)

31. "If you were a box of cereal, what cereal would you be, and why?" (My answer would be bite-sized Shredded Wheat—heart healthy, with no added cholesterol, sugars, saturated fat, trans fat, or sodium.)

32. "If there were a movie about your life, who would play you and why?" (My answer would be Tom Hanks (Forrest Gump)—who was nice guy, a bit naive, enjoyed fitness/running, and was highly successful despite numerous setbacks in life.)

Franklin's "Stepping out of the Box" Concluding Question(s). To make my interviews somewhat memorable or unique, I'll usually challenge the candidate with one or more unconventional questions, seven of which are listed in the following, which usually evoke a smile at the end of the interview and may provide me with some additional insight on how they approach unconventional or thought-provoking queries or scenarios:

1. Connect the "Nine Dots" using four straight lines without taking your pen off the paper.
   (See Figure 9.1.)

2. Look familiar? Where have you seen this letter sequence before?
   QWERTYUIOP

3. What word, when adding "er" to it, makes it shorter?

4. What "flower" best describes the "space" between your nose and your chin?

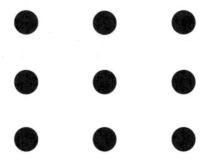

FIGURE 9.1

5. Listed below is the Roman numeral IX. Can you add just one mark or symbol to this Roman numeral and change it to the number 6?

IX

6. Look at this box for a moment. What does it say?

LEAVES
ON THE
THE
GROUND

7. Think unconventionally! Provide the best solution to the brainteaser listed below:

You're driving alone in your two-seat convertible (top up) on a stormy night. At a bus stop you see three people. One is an elderly woman who's obviously seriously ill and needs immediate medical attention. One is an old friend. The third person, a recent acquaintance, is the man or woman of your dreams—that soul mate you've waited for all your life.

Now, here's the part you have to think about: Only one passenger will fit in your car. Which? How would you handle this?

Answers:

1. (See Figure 9.2.)
2. The top line of letters on your computer keyboard
3. Short   short plus "er" = shorter

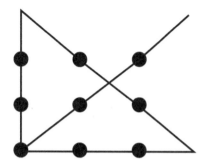

FIGURE 9.2

4. Tulips
5. Add an "S" before the IX, i.e., SIX
6. LEAVES ON THE THE GROUND. Do you really see what you look at? Most people don't really focus on what they see and are not very observant.
7. Ask your old friend to drive the elderly "sick" woman to the nearest hospital and remain at the bus stop with the man or woman of your dreams.

THE STRANGE WAY WE READ?

AMAZING ORDER OF LETTERS

Aoccdrnig to a rscheearer at Cmabridge Uinervtisy, it deosn't mttaer in waht oredr the ltteers in a wrod are, the olny iprmoantt tihng is that the frist and lsat ltteer be at the rghit pclae.

The rset can be a total mses and you can sitll raed it wouthit porbelm.

Tihs is bcuseae the huamn mnid deos not raed ervey lteter by istlef, but the wrod as a wlohe.

Amzanig huh?

Can You Identify the Superachievers Listed Below?

Orpah Wfniery	Jfef Bzoes	Dyanomd Jhon	Rerobt Haveerjc
Mrak Cbuan	Dlloy Ptraon	Aelde Akdins	Mrak Zcukererbg
Blil Geats	Ncik Sbaan	Sevetn Sbpielreg	Bbarara Crorcoan
Mihcllee Oabma	Maehcil Jradon	Lbeorn Jmeas	Tnoy Bnetent
Tahoms Bdray	Lroi Grnieer	Kvien O'earLy	Rarichd Bsorann

10

---

*Be a Connector: The Power
of Positive Associations,
Collaborations, and Relationships*

It's not where you go or who you go with—it's who you might meet when you get there.

Heloise

THE MOST POWERFUL STRATEGY TO
IMPROVE YOUR PERFORMANCE?

Surround yourself with people who personify the qualities you seek—and you'll thrive. Specifically, people who will push and challenge you to become a world class tennis player, a preeminent lawyer, physician, or professor, or a game-changing scientist or researcher. The company you keep becomes a critical factor in your future success. Strive to work with and learn from "the best"—and let your competition work with "the rest."

The dividends of hanging around people you'd like to emulate are exemplified by the story of John Assaraf, a highly successful multi-millionaire whose *early* experiences and study of human potential provided him with an understanding of the laws and principles that superachievers embrace. Although John grew up in a home that was filled with an abundance of love, money was a recurring issue—specifically, the lack of it. Early on, he joined a small group of neighborhood kids who

DOI: 10.4324/9781003260387-12

were adept at shoplifting and other petty crimes. However, his ill-fated direction abruptly changed when he got a job at the Jewish Community Center across the street from his family's apartment. In addition to his $1.65 per hour salary, he was granted access to the men's health club, where he got to know many of the wealthy and highly successful men who hung out there after work. "I received a lot of my early education in the men's sauna," John acknowledged.

His sense of loyalty and gratitude to these men led him to reluctantly return a hundred-dollar bill he found on the floor of the locker room one day to one of the members. For being honest, he was rewarded with a $20 finder fee—but the experience and subsequent lessons he learned from these men were "priceless." This about-face honest act on John's part was the beginning of his education on how the real world operates and how to have anything you want in life by following the laws and principles of success, wealth, trust, integrity, honesty, exceeding people's expectations, and building relationships—*things that were never taught in school.* Additional lessons the men taught him included: Regardless of your race, color, age, or socioeconomic status, never give up on pursuing your dreams; stop complaining about your situation; become laser-focused on achieving your life's goals and dreams; and, nothing is more important than having a positive self-image. He parlayed this knowledge into herculean achievements in real estate, internet software, personal growth, and business coaching, was featured in the book and film *The Secret*, and detailed his journey in his own *New York Times* best-seller *Having It All*.

SURROUND YOURSELF WITH "STARS"

The people you surround yourself with over the years, and those you meet through organizational memberships, business ventures, or networking, can have a profound and favorable impact on your career direction and ultimate success. Accordingly, I strongly recommend that early in your career, you seek out the "stars" in the field that you want to work with (do your homework) and, if at all possible, train under their direction. Observe them carefully, and embrace the personal and professional characteristics that make them stand out. An internship (even a non-paid one) at a place where you'd ultimately love to work can provide a multipurpose steppingstone to career advancement. Once you are out in the workforce, surround yourself with highly educated, hardworking, professional colleagues and support staff who can help you to enhance your knowledge and develop skill sets to increase the likelihood of achieving your goals. Join professional associations in your areas of interest and get active in them to gain exposure to national and international experts in your field, as well as through collaborative research, writing, conferences, and employment opportunities. Finally, as you enter the most productive years of your career, recognize that you've got to give back by mentoring students and younger colleagues. Helping them to achieve their career aspirations will, ironically, help you—and leave a lasting legacy that you'll be proud of.

FIND A MASTER TO LIGHT YOUR CANDLE

A candle is not diminished by giving another candle light.

Earl Nightingale

Hitch your wagon to a star.

Ralph Waldo Emerson

Study anyone who's great, and you'll find that they apprenticed to a master, or several masters. Therefore, if you want to achieve greatness, renown, or superlative success, you must apprentice to a master.

Author, mentor, success guru Robert G. Allen

I learned early in my career that there were tremendous advantages in studying with the "stars" in the field that I wanted to pursue, that is, exercise physiology/science, due to the fact that they were all excellent teachers, research-oriented, and had numerous contacts with nationally and internationally recognized authorities in the field. My specific mentors at Kent State University, the University of Michigan, and Penn State University were Professors Lawrence Golding, Merle Foss, and Elsworth Buskirk, who, collectively, opened my eyes to the extraordinary benefits of being an active member of professional organizations (e.g., the American College of Sports Medicine) and the fundamentals of scientific methods, writing, and research. Subsequently, I studied and collaborated extensively with two giants in the world of cardiology, Drs. Herman K. Hellerstein and Gerald C. Timmis, who helped me immensely improve my writing and presentation skills as well as the art of procuring grant support for future research studies. Over the years, I also learned that my carefully selected mentors demonstrated a common characteristic: All were pleased to generously share their knowledge, wisdom, and experiences with me.

I remember reading that we owe the most, beyond family, to those people who enable and empower us to become what we can become. Whatever knowledge we have acquired has been because of the knowledge, thoughts, and ideas that others before us, who served as our mentors/teachers, managed to assimilate, synthesize, and share. Rather than carrying that knowledge to the grave, they enable us, their students, to use them as our foundation to build upon. Perhaps Sir Isaac Newton summed it up best when he said, "If I can see further, it is by standing on the shoulders of giants." The right early decisions regarding the mentors you surround yourself with can provide enormous dividends to your career in the years that follow.

In summary, review the literature in your particular field. Whose publications, pioneering work, or presentations really resonate with you? Do they have a student internship program, which are common in business and industry and many medical fields? Alternatively, seek out students or junior colleagues who appear destined for success and find out who mentored them. Identify potential mentors who receive high personal and professional ratings. These people may not be in your city or, for that matter, your state. Do your homework! Aim high—and shoot for the "stars." And, don't take "no" for an answer. Early on, find a way to work with the preeminent people in your field.

CONSIDER A STUDENT INTERNSHIP EXPERIENCE

An internship is an official program that is offered by an employer to potential future employees. An intern may work for a designated number of hours per week for a number of months. Undergraduate and graduate students may apply several times throughout the year. Common application requirements include a cover letter, resume, transcript(s), one or two professional letters of recommendation, and potentially, a face-to-face interview. Although there are two types of internships, paid and unpaid, most are unpaid, since the student is primarily there to gain additional real-life knowledge, skills, and abilities to complement their university classroom education. Like finding a job, there are thousands of websites that students can use to find internships. Some of the best internships can be found through networking online (e.g., LinkedIn; Internships.c om). Benefits a student can obtain from participating in an internship include: Gain valuable work experience; explore a particular career path; secure an advantage in the job market; develop specific knowledge, skills, and abilities; establish rapport with potential future employers, clients or patients; network with professionals in the field; gain confidence and invaluable real-life experience; and, transition into a job.

We've used our student internship program at Beaumont Health, which includes rotations in outpatient cardiac rehabilitation, diagnostic stress testing, enhanced external counterpulsation therapy, observation of related cardiac procedures, outpatient consults, written and oral assignments, student presentations, and a weekly lecture series, as a way to train future staff and leaders in the field. We've also found that the internship program is both rewarding and beneficial for our clinical staff, requiring them to maintain continuing education and remain up to date on our policies and procedures via their instructional responsibilities to our student interns. It's been suggested that the best way to learn and continue learning is to regularly attend conferences and teach others.

Lastly, we've come to the sobering realization that *more than 80 percent of our new Beaumont hires, at entry level positions, come from our student intern pools.* People often ask, how do you recruit such outstanding staff? Because we've had the opportunity, over several months, to observe the intern's clinical skills, rapport with staff and patients, professional demeanor, productivity, reliability, and work ethic. When it comes to new hires, I'm a firm believer in the adage, "the past (performance) is prologue to the future." An additional bonus is that when former student interns are hired, limited additional training is required to orient them to the equipment, monitoring techniques, and standard protocols that we employ.

Surround Yourself with 'Stars': The Power of Positive Association

Advertising agency empire-builder David Ogilvy established a tradition of welcoming new executives with a gift of 5 wooden dolls, each smaller than the other, one inside the other. When the recipient finally gets to the 5th little doll, the smallest doll, and opens it, he/she finds this message:

If each of us hires people who are smaller than we are, we shall become a company of dwarfs, but if each of us hires people who are bigger than we are, we shall become a company of giants.

FIGURE 10.1

ENCIRCLE YOURSELF WITH THE BEST AND BRIGHTEST

High achievers typically recruit an extraordinarily talented team of professionals, including associates, manager, administrative support staff, and secretaries, to turn to for assistance, advice, and support (see Figure 10.1). The fact of the matter is that these are the individuals who do the bulk of the work to allow the director to do those things that they enjoy most, and are good at, to further the formidable mission of the company or organization. I've learned that there are people who are good at what I'm not, and love to do what I hate to do. The keys are to find these individuals, treat them with the respect and admiration they deserve, compensate them accordingly, and give them credit for their specific contributions—ideally in front of their colleagues and co-workers. To maintain motivation, morale, and a tireless work ethic, during their yearly performance evaluation, I ask them to rate their overall satisfaction and happiness in the position on a scale from 1 (poor) to 10 (perfect, love the job), taking into account responsibilities, compensation, and feeling that their input and advice are valued and that their contributions are appreciated. Over the years, our ratings have averaged 8.0 to 8.5, with some staff rating their positions as low as 5 and others as high as 12 (☺). For those whose response is "8 or less," I invariably ask what I can personally do to bring that rating up a notch or two at this time next year. This offers the staff member an opportunity to provide me with some constructive feedback to further enhance their satisfaction and to improve the overall workplace environment. These comments (e.g., more responsibility, additional compensation, continuing education opportunities) are written down and systematically followed up on. Finally, it's critically important to consider staff as colleagues and friends, to acknowledge special days or events (birthdays, birth of a child, Christmas gift) and even attend their family funerals, if possible. Teddy Roosevelt once said, "People don't care how much *you* know (and I'd add, 'or what *your* title is' [director, chief, president, CEO]) until they know how much *you* care (about them)." What a great insight!

You can also take the power of positive associations beyond early career mentors and executive and support staff hires. For example, to facilitate partnerships and collaboration with professionals in your field, strongly consider active membership in state and national organizations or associations in your areas of interest. If you can get on committees and/ or the annual program (as a presenter) and begin to surround yourself, get to know, and collaborate with established leaders who are far more well known than you are (e.g., officers in the associations, journal editors, nationally and internationally recognized authorities in your field), you will grow enormously via these professional associations and networking.

THE MAGIC OF ORGANIZATIONAL MEMBERSHIP: A HIGHER CALLING?

Dedicate your life to a cause greater than yourself, and your life will become a glorious adventure.

Mack Douglas

In my early 20s, I pretty much knew what I wanted to do. For me, it became a passion or a crusade, helping middle-aged and older adults prevent or combat chronic disease, especially diabetes, obesity, and cardiovascular disease. I was intrigued by the potential role of lifestyle modification, particularly physical activity, as a preventive health intervention. Clearly, it appeared that there was an educational and research void in addressing these questions—a void that I desperately wanted to help fill.

I shared these sentiments with my advisor at the time, Professor Merle Foss, at the University of Michigan, who responded, "Are you a member of the American College of Sports Medicine or ACSM?" "No," I replied. He said, "You must join and get active in the ACSM—membership will provide *the yellow brick road* to your career goals—follow it!"

He was so right. A pivotal event in my career was joining the ACSM as a student member shortly thereafter (1969) and becoming active in the organization and subsequently, other professional associations, including the American Association of Cardiovascular and Pulmonary Rehabilitation (AACVPR) and the American Heart Association (AHA). Their membership dues were the best investments I ever made! Over the next five decades, my organization/association involvement would lead to service, learning, writing, research, travel, and leadership opportunities I'd never dreamed of, including serving as president of two major professional organizations (ACSM and AACVPR), opening the New York Stock Exchange one morning with the actress Jane Seymour and several AHA leaders, participating in a day media tour on heart disease with the entertainer Donny Osmond, and serving as a visiting professor in Rome, Italy for 2 months. I had no idea of the enormous benefits that organizational membership could provide. Interacting with nationally and internationally renowned professors, scientists, and clinicians who shared my passion for the field—many of whom ultimately became close friends, esteemed colleagues, and collaborators. Not to mention speaking invitations to: Singapore; Reykjavik, Iceland; London, England; Cape Town, South Africa; Jerusalem, Israel; Bangkok, Thailand; Shanghai, China; Rimini, Italy; Sydney, Australia; and, Hong Kong, China—to name just a few. As the Master Card commercial says—*Priceless!*

TOP 10 REASONS TO BE A MEMBER OF A PROFESSIONAL ASSOCIATION(S)

#10 Learn the latest advances in your field

#9 Members/fellows—top authorities in the world

#8 Job hunting/consulting/networking

#7 Publishing/writing/media opportunities

#6 Meet key thought leaders in related fields

#5 Invited presentations (domestic/international)

#4 Opportunities to present at regional/national meetings

#3 Research/grant collaboration

#2 Leadership laboratory

#1 People—friends and esteemed colleagues worldwide

USE COLLABORATION TO EXPONENTIALLY INCREASE YOUR PRODUCTIVITY

Alone we can do so little; together we can do so much.

American author, disability rights advocate Helen Keller

Nobody can achieve success alone.

Educator, life coach, inspirational author Ifeanyi Onuoha

It is the long history of humankind that those who learned to collaborate and improvise most effectively have prevailed.

Charles Darwin

Unity is strength … when there is teamwork and collaboration, wonderful things can be achieved.

American poet Mattie Stepanek

Collaboration occurs when two individuals or a group of people work together toward achieving a common goal or answering a question by sharing their ideas, experiences, and skills. Elements of successful collaboration include: Establish clear definitions and agreements on the roles of colleagues or team members in the collaborative process; keep communication open within groups by readily sharing the information necessary to carry out assignments; reach consensus about goals and methodologies for completing projects or tasks; offer recognition of, respect for, and credit for the contributions of all collaborators; identify obstacles to progression or productivity and address these challenges cooperatively as they occur; place group goals above personal satisfaction/

recognition, especially if you are the leader; and, apologize for missteps and avoid holding grudges over the mistakes of other team members. Outstanding leaders (and coaches) will often personally take responsibility for setbacks, stating they should have done a better job in preparing the group or in clarifying the tasks and responsibilities at hand, but credit the team or entire group for the successes that occur. Noteworthy examples of teamwork and collaboration in the movie and publishing industries are detailed in the following.

> *The Spielberg/Lucas Dynamic Duo.* I'm a huge fan of the blockbuster movie director Steven Spielberg. Several years ago, in a television interview, he was asked, "Mr. Spielberg, you're a genius. How do you do all these great movies?" Spielberg responded that he surrounds himself with extraordinary people who have skills, abilities, and resources that he doesn't have—"George Lucas, for example, his technologic wizardry makes me (as the director) look great. Thus, if I'm approached to direct a movie, and I really like the script and feel it can't be magnificently done, to my satisfaction, without George, I'll tell them you've got to hire two guys for this movie, Steven Spielberg and George Lucas (and his talented crew)."
>
> Spielberg's response substantiated the fact that effective partnering enables you to remove the limits of your existing resources and infinitely multiplies your potential. It highlights two essential, learnable skills for any of us to employ when seeking partners for a given project. First, to identify and recruit the right partners, that is, highly talented people who can provide unique complementary skills to fill a current void in our existing resources—as well as people we are confident that we can amicably work with. Second, to effectively utilize the independent and additive knowledge and skills that they bring to the task at hand, and to motivate and support them accordingly, by providing them the acknowledgment, recognition, resources, and generous compensation (if appropriate) they deserve in helping to bring the project to fruition.
>
> *Evolution of the Chicken Soup for the Soul® series.* Another example is the legendary partnership that developed between Jack Canfield and Mark Victor Hansen on the *Chicken Soup for the Soul®* books. Canfield strongly felt there was a need for, and that people in the United States

and worldwide would embrace, a unique book series that included true, uplifting, motivational, and inspirational stories that he had read or others had conveyed to him over the years. While he was sharing his plan of action over breakfast one day with a friend and colleague, Mark Victor Hansen, Hansen said he loved the idea and that he would welcome the opportunity to collaborate on the book. Canfield acknowledged that the book was already half written, but Hansen persisted, highlighting the fact that he could write and provide many additional stories, and that his networking contacts, promotional style, and marketing expertise would be a huge plus for the project. The deal that was consummated and the synergy that was created by that one casual conversation truly represents an approach for countless others to emulate. Today, with the assistance of many co-authors, thousands of contributors, and a large support staff, the *Chicken Soup for the Soul®* book series has now generated over 250 titles that have been published in more than 100 countries, and more than 500 million copies have been sold worldwide! Combining the skill sets of two relatively unknown authors, who were recognized in only a couple of narrow fields, led to both being internationally recognized and to a cascade of writing, licensing, and self-help online and seminar materials worth tens of millions of dollars in royalties and ancillary income.

Academics/Research: Collaboration Enhances Reputation. Early descriptive or observational research studies conducted by one or two individuals have evolved to large-scale contemporary investigations (e.g., randomized controlled trials), requiring a team of researchers with varied expertise that includes: direct data collection; formulating computerized databases; methodologic design; statistical analysis; writing skills; and, serial grant procurement. Many of these large-scale, multimillion-dollar trials involve thousands of subjects, undergoing extensive baseline and follow-up studies, to determine outcomes over years. In the same way as the old adage posits, "It takes a village to raise a child," it also takes a village to conduct groundbreaking clinical and scientific studies. Accordingly, the average number of authors per cited articles by MEDLINE and PubMed increased from 1.5 in 1950 to 5.8 per publication in 2020. Today, many large-scale trials published in big-name scientific/clinical journals include 10 to 25 or more co-authors. Collaboration is the name of the game!

When I applied for my position as director of cardiac rehabilitation at William Beaumont Hospital in 1985, I vividly remember an interchange I had with one of the co-directors of cardiology, Dr. Gerald Timmis, during the interview process when I posed the question: "In addition to my work with patients, specifically diagnostic studies, treatment interventions, and education/counseling, what areas would you want me to prioritize?" Responsibilities I suggested included: teaching, community service, media interviews, procuring research grants, research, publishing, mentoring staff, residents, and cardiology fellows, giving national and international invited presentations, conference organization, serving on committees, administrative work (e.g., staff training, formulating policies and procedures, staff evaluations, interviewing for new potential hires), reviewing for journals (editorial board appointments), service to major professional organizations (i.e., AHA, ACSM, AACVPR), and outreach to the philanthropic community. I'll never forget Dr. Timmis' response: "All the above. Put us on the map!" He also added that he would expect me to serve as a co-author on the book he edited and updated each year, *Cardiovascular Review*, a summary of the world literature in cardiovascular disease. I came to the sobering realization that this position, which (by the way) included a 50 percent raise, was an extraordinary opportunity, one that I could not pass up. It would also require a 7 days per week commitment (working at home in the evenings and weekends), which my wife Linda and I accepted.

How was I going to get all these things done—and done well?! I realized that one person can't be great at everything and wanted to focus on those responsibilities I was particularly good at and enjoyed doing. In a nutshell, it involved recruiting a superb support staff, people I could count on, and embracing the role of teamwork and collaboration in virtually every aspect of my job responsibilities. Recruited foundational support staff included a superb administrative secretary, Brenda White, and a graphic artist par excellence, Sue Tomasczyki, to help with manuscripts/correspondence/communications and slides/illustrations, respectively! As a voracious collector of famous inspirational and motivational quotes, six seemed particularly relevant to the initial and subsequent challenges that I faced in this role. These included:

"We" multiplies the power of "I."

Author Aniekee Ezekiel

Teamwork is the best investment.
Inspirational writer Israelmore Ayivor

If you can dream it, you can team it.
Best-selling author Richie Norton

Teamwork makes the dream work
Author Bang Gae

It is literally true that you can succeed best and quickest by helping others to succeed.
Napoleon Hill

Find a group of people who challenge and inspire you, spend a lot of time with them, and it will change your life.
American actress, comedian, writer Amy Poehler

What else did I do that worked well? I increasingly began to view every encounter that I had with acquaintances, colleagues, and associates as an "opportunity." If they were working on something that appealed to me, I wouldn't hesitate to say, "I'd love to be involved with you with that publication, book, conference, etc. with the experience and skills that I have in ...." Almost invariably, they'd say, "Yes, it would be great to have you involved." Similarly, on projects or publications I was working on, I'd contact colleagues and invite them to be co-authors or collaborators, with the understanding that I'd be doing the heavy lifting on this one. I quickly learned that people generally respond in kind. Oftentimes, they reciprocated by inviting me to collaborate on a writing project that they were initiating, or alternatively, with a speaking/conference invitation.

Relative to professional organizations in my areas of interest that I belonged to, I became increasingly involved, and when their leadership asked for volunteers for committee appointments, writing groups, or conference planning, I repeatedly raised my hand. I also agreed to voluntarily review submitted manuscripts for a variety of clinical and scientific journals and worked hard to get my requested comprehensive reviews submitted on time. Many of these led to formal invitations to join the editorial board of these journals or newsletters, resulting in my name being added to the journal's editorial board. Currently, I serve on the editorial board of 15 different scientific and health-related publications.

Partnering to Accomplish More

FIGURE 10.2

Using this simple approach, my professional opportunities skyrocketed over the years, as did my productivity. The rest is history.

In summary, embrace partnering or collaboration in your future career endeavors—share the work, which gets done much faster, share the remuneration (royalties), and share the glory. Ironically, this book is the 27th that I've either written, edited, or co-authored. Almost all of them (23 of the 27) were accomplished by working with other authors or editors. This one, which by the way took *years* to write, was an individual effort (i.e., sole author). The point I'm making? If you want to get something done faster, partner with others rather than going it alone (see Figure 10.2).

MENTORING PAYS BOOMERANG DIVIDENDS

Peter Drucker wrote: "High achievement seldom accrues to a man or woman who has not been inspired by a mentor; the word mentor means wise and trusted counselor." He/she can be a parent, a schoolteacher, a college professor, a director—anyone who represents what we most want to become.

The *Harvard Business Review* said that "Everyone who makes it has a mentor." Similarly, Lee Iacocca said, "You've got to have mentors along the way."

Eric Hoffer expounded, "Those who invest themselves in becoming all they can become and, more important than that, those who invest themselves in helping others become all they can become, are involved in the most important work on the face of the earth." We should never forget that mentors set an example for others to emulate, and that the flame of their candle is sustained and potentially everlasting when it is used to light other candles (i.e., their students) who continue this practice.

I tell my students that individuals who've already successfully done what you want to do are available and out there—you simply have to find them and see if they might be willing to serve as your mentor. In my experience, most highly successful people are more than willing to share with the younger generation the skills, strategies, and secrets that enabled them to accomplish their goals.

In mentoring countless students over the years, I've also learned that the more you help other people succeed in life (i.e., their career), the more they will want to reciprocate, sometimes years later, by "lifting you up." There is no mystery and nothing selfish about it—it's just a matter of cause and effect. Remember Ampere's laws of attraction. Like begets like. Doing something for others will bring about a willingness on their part to do something for you—and oftentimes the dividends are disproportionate, come unexpectedly, or both.

Finally, be eager to return the favor, in some way, shape, or form, to the mentor who believed in you. As your career flourishes, make the time to light the candle of others by serving as their mentor. In doing so, you'll lay the foundation for your legacy and maintain the momentum and motivation that your mentor instilled in you.

THE CLYDESDALE TEAMWORK ANALOGY

In closing, certainly you've seen the Budweiser beer commercials around Christmas time—those featuring the magnificent Clydesdale horses? What you may not know is that a single Clydesdale horse can pull a load up to 8,000 pounds. So, what happens when we harness two of these horses together? Well, you might assume they can pull 16,000 pounds, right? Wrong. Two Clydesdales working together can actually pull 24,000 pounds, three times as much weight as either working individually. But there's more! If the two horses have been trained as a team and worked in tandem before, some reports suggest as much as 32,000 pounds could be moved, or four times the weight that either horse could pull on their own.

Similarly, people working together can create outputs or productivity exponentially higher and of superior quality than either one could generate on their own. The ultimate career advice? If you're striving for innovation, embrace partnerships and collaboration. Two or more people with complementary skills working toward a common goal represent one of the greatest quests in all of human endeavor, the ultimate thrill ride. Don't miss out on the exhilaration that accompanies catching this high-speed career train.

11

Be a People Person: A Crash Course and Self-Help Guide

BELIEVE IT OR NOT?

How important are people skills in getting a job, keeping it, and getting promoted? According to the Stanford Research Institute, 15 percent of the reason you get a job and keep it has to do with technical knowledge and skills. On the other hand, 85 percent of the reason you get a job, keep it, and move up in the organization is people skills and people knowledge.

A strong set of must-know people skills will empower you to create awesome relationships with those around you, enabling you to achieve a high degree of success in anything you do. Ask chief executive officers (CEOs) of Fortune 500 companies their *#1 consideration in hiring/ promoting people*, and they'll tell you "the ability to work with people." What are they looking for? People of integrity (who do what they say…), people who shower their employees and/or co-workers with praise and appreciation, people who are generous with their time and support, and individuals who are simply nice people.

In his masterful book, *Smile and Succeed for Teens*, Kirt Manecke highlights essential people skills for today's wired world that apply to all ages, which are summarized and amplified below. When teaching these, I refer to them as "People Skills: The Sweet 16." Under each category, I've included one or more famous relevant quotes that further highlight the significance of each of these in your people skills armamentarium.

DOI: 10.4324/9781003260387-13

PEOPLE SKILLS: THE SWEET 16

#1 SMILE AND THE WORLD SMILES WITH YOU

The person who is smart enough to keep smiling usually winds up with something good enough to smile about. A smile adds "face value."

American businessman, author, and columnist Harvey Mackay

Smiling can be a competitive advantage—it makes every person feel a little better, and every situation a little brighter.

Richard Branson

It costs nothing but creates much. It enriches those who receive, without impoverishing those who give. It happens in a flash and the memory of it sometimes lasts forever. None are so rich they can get along without it, and none so poor but are richer for its benefits. It creates happiness in the home, fosters good will in a business, and is the countersign of friends. It is rest to the weary, daylight to the discouraged, sunshine to the sad, and Nature's best antidote for trouble. Yet it cannot be bought, begged, borrowed, or stolen, for it is something that is no earthly good to anybody till it is given away. And if in the last-minute rush of the business-day, some of our colleagues should be too tired to give a smile, may we ask you to leave one of yours. For nobody needs a smile so much as those who have none left to give!

Anonymous

#2 MAINTAIN GOOD EYE CONTACT
(Note: If you feel that you are staring at the person you are interacting with, look at their nose [for real]).

Van Gogh couldn't have painted the stars in your eyes.

Author Nina Mouawad

The eyes are so telling. That's how you engage with people and bond with them. I love direct, strong eye contact.

American makeup artist and entrepreneur Huda Kattan

When I was interviewing Hillary Clinton, I knew when I'd ask her something that she wasn't going to give me the complete truth because she would break eye contact with me.

English photographer and author Amanda de Cadenet

#3 LEAVE YOUR ELECTRONIC DEVICES OFF OR SILENCED

The best way to "kill" an interview, is to have your phone ringing during it.
Barry Franklin

The person in front of you is more important than your phone.
Actress and singer Amy Chan

#4 SAY "PLEASE," "THANK YOU," AND "YOU'RE WELCOME"
(Note: These are just as important over the phone and online as they are face-to-face.)

To say "thank you" or "please" is to empower the other individual for choosing to take action versus being told to take action (and having no power).
Former analyst at Wells Fargo and media personality Shaurja Ray

#5 SHAKE HANDS FIRMLY
(Note: Always in a standing position; if appropriate, stand up.)

Initiate a proper handshake and the whole world opens up to you.
Chairman, Savvy Turtle clothing company, James D. Wilson

You could approach someone worlds apart from you by offering them, like a handshake, a simple truth from their own lives.
Canadian author Danielle Bennett

#6 TAKE THE LEAD BY INTRODUCING YOURSELF TO OTHERS

The only way to make a friend is to be one.
Ralph Waldo Emerson

#7 PAY ATTENTION TO PEOPLE: LISTEN CAREFULLY

The word "listen" contains the same letters as "silent."
Austrian classical pianist, poet, and author Alfred Brendel

(Note: To improve your listening skills, get in the habit of summarizing [in a nutshell] the information that a person has conveyed to you immediately back to them.)

#8 BE ENTHUSIASTIC—IT'S CONTAGIOUS, JUST LIKE A SMILE

The real secret of success is enthusiasm.
Automotive industry executive Walter Chrysler

Nothing great was ever achieved without enthusiasm.
Ralph Waldo Emerson

#9 GENERALLY ASK OPEN-ENDED QUESTIONS, UNLESS YOU'RE REALLY BUSY
(Note: These questions begin with Who, What, When, Where, Why, or How, and can't be answered with a "Yes" or "No.")

Asking the right questions takes as much skill as giving the right answers.
Pioneer of professional staffing services Robert Half

#10 USE POSITIVE BODY LANGUAGE
(Note: To convey confidence, a positive attitude, and a professional demeanor, avoid crossed arms, slouched posture, or looking down.)

Respect yourself and others will respect you.
Confucius

#11 MAKE A MISTAKE? APOLOGIZE AND MEAN IT
(Note: Be specific about what you are sorry for; don't just say "sorry" or "my bad.")
An apology is the superglue of life. It can repair just about anything.
Cartoonist Lynn Johnston

#12 GREET PEOPLE BY NAME
(Note: Use titles [e.g., Mr., Mrs., Dr., Judge, Professor] as a preface to the person's last name, unless they instruct you otherwise [e.g., please call me by my first name].) There is a section on Remembering Names later in this chapter.

"EVERYBODY KNOWS YOUR NAME"

Sometimes you wanna go
Where everybody knows your name

And they're always glad you came
You wanna be where you can see
Our troubles are all the same
You wanna be where everybody knows
your name

**Cheers Theme Songwriters Gary Portnoy & Judy
Hart-Angelo**

#13 PREPARE, PREPARE, PREPARE

(Note: If you follow this advice for everything you do in life, you'll be miles ahead of your competition. Got an important meeting, presentation, teleconference, or interview? Don't wing it. Do your preparation ahead of time.)

By failing to prepare, you are preparing to fail.

Benjamin Franklin

Before anything else, preparation is the key to success.

Alexander Graham Bell

Champions do not become champions when they win the event, but in the hours, weeks, months, and years they spend preparing for it. The victorious performance itself is merely the demonstration of their championship character.

Actor Alan Armstrong

It usually takes me more than three weeks to prepare for a good impromptu speech.

Mark Twain

#14 LOOK THE PART: DRESS FOR SUCCESS

(Note: Yes, people do judge a book by its cover. Grooming also counts!)

First impressions occur instantly or within two seconds.

Malcolm Gladwell

You never get a second chance to make a good first impression.

Will Rogers

#15 NEVER COMPLAIN, NEVER EXPLAIN, AVOID GOSSIP

(Note: You are almost always on stage. Avoid making negative, unprofessional comments or gossiping about others. These actions can undermine the trust, unity, or morale of a group … make us seem negative and/or disloyal … and cause those around us to pay less heed when we voice more important concerns in the future. Only listen to complaints that appear to be justified [e.g., those that could compromise staff or customers]. Keep conversations professional.) According to www.wordscanheal.org, the secret to avoiding gossip is not to think badly of other people. What you think and feel inevitably comes out in your speech.

Great minds discuss ideas; average minds discuss events; small minds discuss people.

Eleanor Roosevelt

One stops being a child when one realizes that telling one's troubles does not make things better.

Italian novelist Cesare Pavese

Blaming is an excuse to do nothing about reality—an excuse not to take action.

Self-help author Andrew Matthews

Never explain—your friends do not need it, and your enemies will not believe you anyway.

American writer, publisher and philosopher Elbert Hubbard

#16 MASTER ELECTRONIC ETIQUETTE

(Note: Your communications, including texting, sending emails, and using social media, are reflections of your professionalism. Use proper English, complete sentences, spell out words, include proper salutation [greeting, closing remarks], and say "please," "thank you," and "you're welcome." Proofread and spell-check before sending or posting. Remember: Brevity is a virtue.)

Shouting is never professional. Avoid ALL CAPS.

Kirt Manecke

In addition to these basic people skills that are requisites for success in virtually any field, I'd like to share with you some insightful, motivational, and inspirational stories and lessons that I've compiled on *21 additional success secrets*, in an easy-to-use format, each including a success message that you can adopt and apply in your own life. These represent the perspectives of some of the world's greatest thinkers, plain old common sense, and empiric experiences on how to win friends, influence people, and build self-esteem. The stories and events included in this section may hold the key to helping you better clarify your purpose in life and how to accomplish it with energy, enthusiasm, and overwhelming success.

In *The Wizard of Oz*, Dorothy was advised by Glinda, the Good Witch of the North, to follow *the yellow brick road* to find the renowned Wizard, who could help her to return to Kansas (the destination she desperately wanted). I'm confident that the writings and messages contained in this section will help you illuminate and adeptly navigate your *yellow brick road* to get from where you are to where you want to be.

Patience and Persistence Are Virtues. Philosopher and writer Joseph de Maistre said, "To know how to wait is the great secret of success." Regardless of the accomplishment, an invariable forerunner is patience—patience with others, with those on whom we are dependent or reliant, and with ourselves. If your goal or aspiration has not yet materialized, keep at it, and be patient.

The corollary of patience is persistence, another secret of success. Successful people have come to realize that it is the main ingredient in winning at anything. *Warning*: The universe often seems to be testing us, in what's known as the "eleventh hour" principle, to see if we are really serious about attaining our goal. Don't be deceived! According to Andrew Matthews, the "eleventh hour," when everything before us looks darkest, coldest, and bleak, is oftentimes a harbinger of future opportunities and overwhelming success. But if you hang on long enough, it could be time to rejoice.

Get Rid of Negative Thoughts or Emotions: Forgive Others. Harmful emotions like anger, resentment, hatred, holding grudges, animosity, jealousy, revenge, self-pity, guilt, and remorse only drag *you* down, redirecting your focus and attention from your goals, dreams, and aspirations. While you cannot change the past, harboring these feelings is deleterious to your health, well-being, and productivity. When we withhold forgiveness, we suffer. The decision to forgive yourself or somebody else is your affirmation to live in the present. You'll be better off for it. Perhaps the tagline in the film *Donnie Brasco* summed it up best: "Forget about it." The winners in life live in the present and strive for strength of purpose, strength of mind, and strength of character.

> Anger is an acid that can do more harm to the vessel in which it is stored than to anything on which it is poured.
>
> **Mark Twain**

> Resentment is like drinking poison and waiting for it to kill your enemy.
>
> **Nelson Mandela**

> Keeping score of old scores and scars, getting even and one-upping, always makes you less than you are.
>
> **Malcolm Forbes**

Silence Is Golden. As a general rule, avoid conflicts due to varying opinions (e.g., political preferences). *Let the other person have the right to his/her belief or sentiments.* At a minimum, don't respond so negatively that it makes resolution difficult, embarrassing, or awkward—particularly when others are present. The best response is usually silence. You won't make any mistakes with your mouth shut.

> Speak when you are angry, and you'll make the best speech you'll ever regret.
>
> **Lawrence J. Peter**

> Try to avoid falling out with people. The world is a very small place.
>
> **Richard Branson**

WARREN BUFFETT: WISEST COUNSEL I EVER RECEIVED?

It was from a Berkshire Hathaway board member and it boiled down to exercising restraint and humility. He told me: "You can tell a guy to go to hell tomorrow—you don't give up the right. But keep your mouth shut today, and see if you feel the same way tomorrow."

Why such sage advice? Because the person you did not tell off or offend today may be in a position to "open up a door" for you tomorrow, or in the near future, BUFFETT learned.

Take Home Message? This applies to your phone calls, text messages, emails and snail mails. If you would be offended by your remarks, don't send them to others. Silence is golden!

Integrity: The #1 Quality for Success. To me, integrity has always meant doing what you say you are going to do. However, the quality also includes a person's mindset and character in doing the right things by putting people first. *Put people first and profit last*; the more you embrace this business practice, the more successful and profitable you'll become! Someone once wrote that if honesty didn't exist, it ought to be invented as the fastest way of getting rich. Why? Because you never have to correct the truth. Moreover, clients, customers, and patients gravitate to those they trust.

As a health researcher, I'm well aware of landmark studies that have unequivocally shown that lifelong cigarette smoking reduces the lifespan by 10 to 12 years, on average. Yet, because the habit is addicting and highly profitable, cigarettes continued to be sold by countless stores throughout the country, including pharmacies—until Larry Merlo, president/CEO, announced that CVS pharmacy, the second largest drugstore chain, would stop selling cigarettes and all tobacco products at its more than 7,600 stores nationwide by October 1, 2014. The media release stated:

> Ending the sale of cigarettes and tobacco products at CVS/pharmacy is simply the right thing to do for the good of our customers and our company. The sale of tobacco products is inconsistent with our purpose—helping people on their path to better health.

Their overall revenues plummeted—right? Wrong! CVS revenues actually increased by almost 10 percent, as their lost cigarette revenues were more than offset by strong pharmacy sales. Why? I believe that the vast majority of the U.S. adult population, approximately 80 percent, who were non-smokers (like me), perceived CVS as a company with integrity, and one that they (and I) decided to increasingly support in the future. The bottom line? *Integrity is a priceless quality that invariably leads to overwhelming success in the long run.*

Laughter and Smiling Are Wonderfully Therapeutic. Earl Nightingale said, "I have found it a good rule of thumb to be highly suspicious of anyone who takes himself too seriously." He went on to suggest that cruel people didn't seem to be able to see anything funny in the world. Dictators or "wannabe" dictators are also widely recognized as people who rarely smile or, for that matter, never seem to acknowledge or be able to laugh at themselves or admit their flaws. In contrast, think of the wonderful sense of humor that characterized Mark Twain or Will Rogers, or modern-day comedians Tina Fey, Amy Poehler, Ray Romano, and Ricky Gervais.

I remember reading about a husband who, when he'd had a bad day at the office, would come home with his tie draped over his shoulder. If his wife had had a difficult day, she'd wear her ugly blouse. In either case, these "SOS distress signals" would start them laughing when they met up, with raucous laughter if they'd both had a horrible day. They firmly believed the ritual would clear the air and favorably change their mindset. Accordingly, emotionally healthy people are invariably cheerful, look for the good in people and situations, see a lot of humor in their daily lives, and are able to outwardly laugh at themselves.

Finally, in Norman Cousins' book *Anatomy of an Illness*, he tells how he recovered from a crippling connective tissue disease (ankylosing spondylitis) to resume a healthy, normal life. His main medicine? Massive doses of Vitamin C and daily, self-induced bouts of laughter brought on by old episodes of the television show *Candid Camera* and by various comic films (e.g., Marx Brothers classics). Cousins believed his solemn approach to life had precipitated his illness and hypothesized he could reverse the condition through laughter. He demonstrated what people have said for years, "Laughter is the best medicine."

Make Others Feel Important. The founder of Shake Shack, Danny Meyer, was asked for the keys to his skyrocketing success in the restaurant business. His response? "I see every person I meet with a sign around their neck that reads, 'Make Me Feel Important'," he replied. How does one do that? For starters, during conversations, focus on the other person; that is, let them do the talking and with your open-ended questions, bring the conversation back to *their* ideas and interests. Why open-ended questions (which begin with Who, What, When, Where, Why, or How)? Because they cannot be answered with a simple "yes" or "no" and leave the door open for more conversation.

When most people talk to others, they talk about themselves—and while you're talking they largely tune you out, getting ready to reload to tell you more about themselves. By making the other person feel he or she is important in your eyes, by having them as the central focus during your conversation, you make friends in a hurry. Appear engaged by showing that you're listening; demonstrate empathy, head nodding, and an occasional smile. This approach is also highly effective in bettering human relations and selling your ideas. Oddly enough, the more we listen, the better a conversationalist we seem to the person doing the talking. How do you master the art of communicating with others? In four words: "Listen more, talk less." As a general rule, 70 to 80 percent of the conversation should pertain to *their* likes, interests, and activities. With two ears and one mouth, we should listen more than we talk. It works like a charm, every time!

ALBERT EINSTEIN'S FORMULA FOR SUCCESS

If A is success in life, then $A = x + y + z$.
Work is x; y is play; and z is keeping your mouth shut.

When you listen, you have power. When you talk you give it away.
French Enlightenment writer and philosopher Voltaire

Winning Others Over to Your Side. You can often change others' hostile opinions and gain their support/assistance by agreeing with (or saying you appreciate) their remarks and complimenting them as a preface to expressing your point of view (which may be considerably different from theirs). In addition to backing up what you say with irrefutable facts and logic, if you are trying to win people over to your point of view, empiric experience suggests that it's best to exhibit humbleness of attitude, which is amicably conveyed by prefacing your remarks with some magic words. These may include: "In my opinion," "I may be wrong about this ... but it seems to me ..." or simply "It seems to me ..." This opening does not offend others and suggests that you are open to alternative viewpoints, and if your sentiments are proven wrong, you are not so far out on a limb that you cannot save face. Don't appear too anxious to sell your ideas, avoid using a tone of absolute assuredness, and consider including in your remarks a question, "I've often wondered whether ...?" Using this approach is far less likely to turn people off and potentially sets the stage for those you are speaking with to sell themselves on your ideas.

Give More to Get More. Albert Einstein was once asked, "Why are we here (i.e., put on this earth)?" He turned to his questioner in surprise and replied, "We are here to serve other people." No one can enrich themselves in any way without serving others. The key, however, is to give them more in use value than we receive or charge. Why? People will come back time and time again (and tell their family and friends) about other people, goods, or services when they perceive the value provided far exceeds the cost. On average, Americans tell ~15 other people about a good customer experience. As a result, your business will exponentially expand. Accordingly, you are building a great credit for yourself that will ultimately return via a tidal wave of future dividends, business prosperity, and clients. Known as the "Law of Increase," it is the most common characteristic of all successful people, companies, and services. And to become successful and outstanding at serving others, you don't have to come up with something new. You need only to find ways of doing it better or giving people more than they expected. Using this approach, many unanticipated collaborators, opportunities, and resources will come into your life. The bottom line? If you give more now, you'll get more later.

DELIVER A LITTLE EXTRA TO BOOST CUSTOMER LOYALTY

Jack Welch, the former CEO of General Electric, often said the way to get ahead in business is to deliver what's asked of you to a tee— but then always show up with something more. Specific examples? Double Tree Hotels—give guests warm chocolate chip cookies upon check in. The prize inside Cracker Jack drove more customer loyalty than the core product itself!

Years ago, I started giving a small book on heart health that I had co-authored to every cardiac patient I provided with an educational consult. It cost me a few hundred dollars to do this each year. I told them that I gave it to patients I especially enjoyed meeting with. FYI, I enjoy meeting with every patient I meet.☺ Many patients offer to pay for the book or return it—which I decline. Invariably, my consults are among the most highly rated in our department. Perhaps it's due, in part, to the generous amount of time I spend with them, or more likely because they leave the consult with far more than they expected.

Winners in life do what is required, and a little bit more.
Arthur L. Williams, Jr.

Appreciate and Be Grateful for What You Have. When you live by this adage, the "law of attraction" suggests you're likely to attract even more good things to reinforce this state of mind. Success guru Anthony Robbins refers to this as "an attitude of gratitude." People who project the most favorable well-being are those who appear happy and content with what they have. They are also the most successful! One of the best ways to convey this is with a smile—whether you are meeting someone face-to-face or even talking with them on the phone. In fact, if you smile as you answer the phone, it favorably modifies the tone of your voice, conveying appreciation and gratitude.

As I discovered more about the power of the subconscious mind, I came to the sobering realization that in order to continue to enjoy good fortune, I needed to feel fortunate. The rationale behind this is that our mind is a magnet, and we gravitate toward what we think about most. In contrast, the person who consistently thinks about what he/she doesn't have will get less and less of what he/she really wants. In summary, if you embrace an "attitude of gratitude" to the world around you, the world projects it back to you, with much more to be grateful for. This aura also conveys an enticing or alluring temperament mistakenly called good luck.

Be the "Master" of Your Actions. Avoid the trap, that is, responding negatively to others who may exhibit rudeness, incivility, or snubs to you or those you may be with. In other words, it's a big mistake, in dealing with others who may exhibit inappropriate behaviors or comments, to respond in kind. If you do, you allow them to unfavorably modify your standard, courteous interchanges with others. When you take the high road, you'll always be perceived as the winner of such unfortunate exchanges and in rare instances, prevent the escalation of an exchange that can result in hazardous outcomes. Throughout this book, I emphasize that people generally respond in kind. This situation, however, represents a notable exception to the rule.

A Three-Pronged Approach to Managing People. Feeling appreciated is the single greatest motivator in the workplace, even exceeding higher wages. First, one of the best ways to enhance the self-esteem and performance of the people around you, including students, co-workers, and staff, is to convey appreciation and praise for a job well done—ideally, in front of others (or in a copied email). In addition, people are more likely to help you achieve your corporate or departmental goals if they believe that you truly appreciate their efforts. It's been said: "Praise to a human being represents what sunlight, water and soil are to a plant—the climate in which they grow best." In my experience as a servant leader for more than four decades, we should take every opportunity to pay a sincere compliment to those on our team. According to Mother Teresa, "People around us are starving for appreciation and acknowledgment, and we have the ability to give them this gift on a regular basis." It costs nothing—and no staff member I've ever worked with has ever complained about being praised too often or feeling overappreciated.

In the early 1950s, Don Clifton, a psychology professor at the University of Nebraska, noted that his field was based almost entirely on examining *what is wrong* with people. Intuitively, he began to wonder if it would be more meaningful to study *what is right* with people and whether positive interactions with others could favorably impact relationships, happiness, productivity, and even success. He emphasized that the results of our encounters with others are rarely neutral; these interactions are almost always positive or negative.

To summarize his research findings, he developed a simple analogy (*The Theory of the Dipper and the Bucket*) to explain the phenomenon. In a nutshell, everyone has an invisible bucket. We are at our best when our buckets are overflowing and at our worst when our bucket is empty. Each of us also has an invisible dipper. During each interaction with others, we can use our dipper to fill or dip from others' buckets. And whenever we choose to fill others' buckets, we in turn fill our own. Why? Because people generally respond in kind. Accordingly, good things happen when people are encouraged, recognized, and praised regularly, and bad things occur in the absence of such positive encounters.

The types of feedback that teachers provide to their students in the classroom also appear to influence learning and performance. Tom Rath and Professor Clifton highlighted a relevant report in their book *How Full Is Your Bucket?* Children in a math class were divided into four groups: Controls, treated in a normal manner; Ignore, the teacher paid no attention to this subset; Criticize, the teacher was very critical of these students' incorrect answers; and Praise, where the teacher was highly complimentary when the students provided accurate responses. At the end of just one week, the group with the highest math test scores (problems solved) was the one that routinely received praise. Overall improvements were 5, 19, and 71 percent for the groups that were ignored, criticized, and praised, respectively.

Second, if you are in an administrative or supervisory role, and you are responsible for people, don't tell them how to act with customers; show them by your example.

> You teach what you know, but you reproduce who you are.
>
> **John Maxwell**

> You can preach a better sermon with your actions than with your lips.
>
> **Novelist Oliver Goldsmith**

Thirty years ago, I vividly remember walking down a corridor of our Beaumont Troy Hospital and seeing a young man, neatly dressed in a suit, picking up papers on the floor as he walked in front of me. I asked the doctor I was with who was the guy in the suit "doing the housekeeping chores" for the hospital. Oh, that's Mr. Michalski, he replied, our new assistant hospital administrator. I met Mr. Michalski later that day and commented to him that it was refreshing to see his actions in the hospital hallway. "Why not, we're all responsible for keeping our hospital clean," he replied. That day, I adopted his example and have practiced it ever since! (Footnote: Mr. Michalski retired a few years ago as the CEO and president of the entire Beaumont Health System. For his pioneering leadership and exemplary service, upon his retirement, the Beaumont Board awarded him a very generous parting bonus for bringing Beaumont together with two other major healthcare systems in the area. An extraordinary career with a storybook ending—but for me, it all started with watching a young man, impeccably dressed, picking up papers from a hospital corridor floor, a habit that I subsequently embraced by his example.)

DON'T TELL PEOPLE: SHOW THEM

Effective leaders exemplify the behaviors that they want to see in others (i.e., trust, integrity, kindness, humility, graciousness).

True Story. Ray Kroc, the founder of McDonald's, was known by his employees for picking up cigarette butts in the parking lots of his restaurants, setting the tone for cleanliness and substantiating McDonald's mantra—"Never be satisfied."

Finally, if you are managing people, avoid making critical comments, and carefully frame constructive criticism so that staff don't take it personally or become offended. In my experience with yearly performance evaluations, a supervisor can highlight 10 attributes or performance pluses and offer one critical comment, and the employee will leave the office depressed, focused on the latter. For example, rather than stating that an individual could make better use of their time, reframe the constructive comment to state they should write down the key tasks they need to complete each day, prioritize them, and complete unfinished tasks the following day, as well as new assignments. Perhaps an even better approach during a performance evaluation would be to ask the employee to highlight their strengths and areas to improve on. Regarding the latter, they may bring up the challenge of getting things done, which gives you the opportunity to agree with them, even reiterate that this is a common challenge among staff, and provide some constructive suggestions in this regard. *In summary, withholding praise is 10 times more effective than criticism.* Praise those around the person who is not doing as well. In my experience, underperformers will want to be praised and will often step up their game.

> You get the best effort from others, not by lighting a fire beneath them, but by building a fire within.
> **Best-selling author, management trainer Bob Nelson**

Niceness Trumps Importance. I had the wonderful opportunity to work with a highly professional, multi-talented African American woman named Shay Kennedy at the national American Heart Association (AHA), who taught me an important lesson in life. Shay uniquely worked with AHA staff and many volunteers around the United States, including high-level, hardworking, highly successful physicians, clinicians, researchers, academics, company presidents, and CEOs of major companies who also sat on the AHA Board of Trustees. I remember attending several of the Board meetings, where someone might whisper to another, oh, that's

Dr./Professor so-and-so from Harvard, or the CEO of ..., or the media personality in New York. I asked Shay a question one time on how she adeptly works with this high-powered group of very important people. She smiled at my question and responded: "Dr. Franklin, at the bottom of every email I send is a statement that I live by and highly endorse—'It's nice to be important; however, it is more important to be nice' (to people)." Shay added that the preeminent AHA volunteers she works with are, in fact, very nice. I believe that's, in part, why they are so successful. They embrace *the Golden Rule*—treating others as they themselves would like to be treated. In the Jewish faith, we refer to such people, that is, those with honor and integrity, as mensches. I'm convinced that if you take two people who are comparable in talent and abilities, the decent and responsible person is the one who's going to get the job, contract, or in this case, the AHA Board position.

In summary, being nice wields amazing power. Nice people are more productive workers, more effective leaders, more likely to have enduring marriages, and less likely to find themselves in court. Such people commonly demonstrate small acts of kindness, share, or confer the credit on others and freely offer compliments to support staff and associates. *The fact of the matter is that people automatically like you when you treat them with respect, consideration, and interest (in them).* Remember, when everything else is equal, management promotes the people it likes; so, be nice and enjoy the ride to the top!

WANT SOMEONE'S TIME AND ATTENTION? BE NICE

I've conducted an informal study and came to a sobering realization. ADMISSION: I spend, on average, 5 to 10 more minutes during my educational consults with nice patients as compared with their grumpy counterparts. Whenever possible, preface your meeting with a compliment. I vividly remember a meeting I had with a new heart patient and his wife. She opened the conversation with "Dr. Franklin, you are famous. It's a pleasure to meet you. I've seen you on TV, quoted in the newspapers, and heard many wonderful things about you over the years." I ended up giving them a book and spending 50 minutes with them (perhaps subconsciously to prove what they had heard about me was true).

You Cannot Know Too Many People. I'm convinced that doors or opportunities in life open up for us because of things we did or that others do for us. Essentially, we live out our dreams because of our achievements and/or doors that were opened up for us by all sorts of extraordinary people (e.g., role models, professors, mentors, supervisors, family, friends) we meet along the way. Unfortunately, most people tend to speak to another only after the other person has spoken or smiled first. We are reactive rather than proactive. Reminds me of the man who sat in front of the fireplace and said, "Give me heat, and then I'll add wood to get the fire going." The world just doesn't work that way. Be nice, be polite, and smile, and don't be afraid to introduce yourself to someone you would like to know. More than 90 percent of the time, smiling and saying hello first broadens our horizons, adds to our network of acquaintances and friends, and sometimes leads to contacts and opportunities we never dreamed of. Focus on what you have in common. One example? I met a man, years ago, sitting next to me in business class on a Northwest Airlines (now Delta) flight. Our conversation, which I initiated, revealed that he was a vice president for the airline, second in charge. Long story short? My difficulty in periodically upgrading from economy class to business class (using frequent flyer miles) on international flights had now been resolved. (More on this story later in the book.) The individual who shuts others out of his/her life ends up limiting the doors that can sometimes be opened by complete strangers who become acquaintances or even friends. Being a loner decreases the likelihood of your success. *You cannot know too many people. Moreover, never miss an opportunity to say something nice about them.*

LIMITLESS FRIENDSHIPS LEAD TO UNBOUNDED OPPORTUNITIES

The more people you know, and the more likeability and sociability you convey, the better your odds of becoming lucky in life. Malcolm Gladwell calls these types of people "connectors." These people interact with large groups of influential people, who, in turn, invariably share information, contacts, and opportunities.

Don't Criticize Others. People know when they've made an error, or could have handled something better, and they know that you know it too.

No need to bring it to their attention, and when you refrain from making a critical comment, either face to face, on the phone (voice or text), or via a nasty email, they're grateful and appreciate your softer approach. *Don't be a judge or jury to family, friends, staff, or colleagues.* When you feel inclined to criticize others, wait a day, one week, or one month and then, using a New York Italian-Americanism, *fuhgeddaboudit*. Silence is golden. Avoid making the same mistakes I did early in my career.

Keep Climbing, Reaching, and Learning. In the book *Don Quixote*, by Cervantes, the story poses an interesting question: "Why do some men and women discover new vitality and creativity to the end of their days, while others go to seed long before?" To achieve the former, one needs to avoid the fixed attitudes, opinions, and approaches that often characterize middle-aged and older adults. *Keep learning, by setting new goals and aspirations, and be willing to pursue new knowledge, skills, and abilities to bring these to fruition.* Reject stagnation, be inquisitive, and recognize that what you learn that's new, after decades of learning, is what counts the most.

Three "Magic" Words. Years ago, when an American team of mountain climbers conquered Mount Everest, behavioral scientists learned that the replies they gave to answer the same question offered a unique insight regarding individual outcomes. Before the ascent, all of the mountain climbers were asked a series of questions, including "Will you get to the top of Everest?" Although all answered the question with optimism and enthusiasm, the actual responses varied considerably. "That's the goal I plan to achieve," or "I'm going to work at it," or "I'm going to do my best," or "I'm sure going to try," or "I certainly hope to" were among the responses. But the man who was the first to make it to the top confidently and quietly responded to the question with just three words, "Yes, I will." Was this merely a coincidence or a chance finding? I don't think so.

The mindset we embrace before any challenge, whether it is writing a funded research grant, losing 10 pounds, a specific sales goal, or climbing Mount Everest, can be captured by the certainty of your response relative to the likelihood of its achievement. Based on this story, and other anecdotal reports, these three magical words, "Yes, I will," are harbingers of future success. This particular response signifies that more than merely wanting to achieve a goal, you've made up your mind to accomplish it. It highlights the fact that when setting goals, our mindset and our actions to achieve them should be in concert.

The Rx for Happiness? Without question, this mindset goes far beyond some material thing or event that comes into our life that suddenly makes us happy—at least momentarily. "Most people are about as happy as they make up their mind to be," said Abraham Lincoln. It is not what happens to us in life that determines our happiness so much as the way we perceive it. Being happy requires looking for the good in people and situations (see Chapter 3). For example, consider someone who has lost his job. One man sees disaster, whereas another may view it as an opportunity to better himself. Unfortunately, too many people live their life embracing the mantra "I'll be happy when ...." In order to be happier and get more out of life, you simply need to change your thoughts and actions.

> Happiness is something that happens while we are thinking about something else. Those who chase happiness never catch it. Those who spread happiness to others can't escape it.
>
> **Broadcaster, self-help author Mort Crim**

Mort Crim was right—those people who find happiness as a way of life are usually the busiest people, serving others in some way, shape, or form, or those dedicated to a cause greater than themselves (e.g., combatting disease, improving technology, developing safe and effective vaccines, providing needed therapy or rehabilitation, educating people, helping others to become the best that they can be). Other specific strategies include: Cut back on buying things—instead, spend your money on memorable experiences (e.g., vacations); employ yourself (if possible); spend more time with family and friends; volunteer (helping others); and, cultivate a sense of appreciation and gratitude (by giving back). In essence, lasting happiness appears to be conferred on those whose lives are dedicated to making a difference during the flicker of their lifetime. Perhaps the most articulate and comprehensive response I've ever read that addressed this question was offered by John Stuart Mill (1806–1873), a philosopher and economist, who had one of the highest IQs ever reported. Mill said: "Those only are happy who have their minds fixed on some object other than their own happiness: on the happiness of others, or on the improvement of mankind. Aiming thus at something else, they find happiness by the way." Finally, recognize that a smile is a magnet for happiness. Use the following self-assessment scale to rate your current level of happiness and life satisfaction.

LIFE HAPPINESS: SELF-ASSESSMENT SCALE*

Using the 1–7 rating scale below, indicate how much you agree with each of the five statements pertaining to your overall life satisfaction. Total the rating scores for your overall results.

Rating Scale

1	2	3	4	5	6	7
Strongly disagree	Disagree	Slightly disagree	Neither agree nor disagree	Slightly agree	Agree	Strongly agree

Five Statements

1. In most ways, my life is close to my ideal _____
2. The conditions of my life are excellent _____
3. I am satisfied with my life _____
4. So far, I have gotten the important things I want in life _____
5. If I could live my life over, I would change almost nothing _____

Overall Score for Happiness and Life Satisfaction

31–35 = Extremely satisfied
26–30 = Satisfied
21–25 = Slightly satisfied
20 = Neutral
15–19 = Slightly dissatisfied
10–14 = Dissatisfied
5–9 = Extremely dissatisfied

Be a Class Act: Take the High Road. I'm a big fan of the great media work that both Diane Sawyer and Katie Couric have done. Now, I normally don't watch a lot of TV, but I came home one night and saw Diane Sawyer being interviewed, and the interviewer asked her, "Diane, what did you

* Credit: The Satisfaction with Life Scale was developed by Ed Diener, Robert A. Emmons, Randy J. Larsen, and Sharon Griffin.

think of the negative comments that Katie Couric recently had to say about you?" Well, I stopped eating because I wanted to hear what she was going to say. Diane Sawyer replied, "What do you mean?" The interviewer said, "Well, Katie Couric said that you use many of the approaches she employs when talking to her guests—but that you're not a very good interviewer. You don't ask challenging questions to your interviewees and that your style is rather dated." By this time, I'm sitting on the edge of the counter waiting to see what Diane Sawyer is going to say. She must have paused for 20 or 30 seconds, and then replied, "I hadn't heard what you're suggesting that Katie Couric purportedly said about me. It doesn't sound like something that Katie would say about me. And, do I have anything to say? Yes, I think Katie Couric is one of the most talented people in the media business today, and I've always respected and admired her work." That's a class act. Successful people are class acts. *Footnote*: Don't be a victim of Chinese whispers or telephone, a popular children's game. Why? Because errors typically accumulate in the retellings.

Remembering People's Names—A Memorable Demonstration. Many years ago, I vividly recall a medical sales representative at a trade show demonstrating some new equipment that we were interested in potentially purchasing to measure heart-lung fitness during a progressive treadmill test to exhaustion. His computerized system included a two-way mouthpiece and nose clip with tubing that attached to the unit. As I recall, we had between 8 and 10 staff members there that day for the demo. All were dressed in regular clothes, and none were wearing name tags. He asked each staff member he met their name and a question or two, always repeating their name at least once more. We then had the demonstration, and the equipment performed admirably, yielding a high level of aerobic fitness, expressed in units called METs or metabolic equivalents, for the distance runner (subject) who was being tested.

But the most memorable part of the exhibit that day was how he remembered each and every staff member's name as questions arose during and after the demonstration. Afterward, I went up to the sales representative and thanked him for the singularly impressive demo. He replied, "Our technology is way ahead of our closest competitors." "No," I said, I'm referring to your uncanny recall of all of our staff's names during the Q/A," which generated a huge smile on his part. "My mentor trained me well, although I sometimes miss one or two names," he admitted. "Can

I ask the secret?" I replied. "Sure, it's a six-step process, and like anything else, the more you practice it, the better you get," he went on.

NAME RECALL TRICK

#1 Focus on the person; introduce yourself, and ask their first name

#2 Repeat their name aloud

#3 Using their name (aloud), ask them an open-ended question to get them talking; show you are paying attention

#4 As they are answering your question, repeat their name silently (at least 10 times)

#5 Make a visual association between their name and a particular feature (e.g., facial characteristic, hair) or something familiar to you. Perhaps Harry Lorayne, the world's leading expert on memory training, summed it up best: "All we wish to remember must be *associated* with something we already know or remember." For example, I recently met a man who told me to call him Mack. I immediately linked him with the "Golden Arches," *Mc*Donald's

#6 Conclude the interaction by restating their name, e.g., Great to meet you Mack

A person's name is to that person the sweetest and most important sound in any language.

Dale Carnegie

A HARD-TO-PRONOUNCE NAME CAN IMPEDE YOUR SUCCESS

According to one report, lawyers with easy-to-pronounce names became partners more quickly than their counterparts with complex names. Simple-to-say names may help others feel more comfortable with you. In contrast, difficult-to-pronounce names are likely said less often, leading to fewer recommendations and introductions. If your name is unusual, help others become comfortable with it by saying what it rhymes with, or comparing it to something familiar. Example: "Zajonc sounds like science, but starts with a Z." Also, look for opportunities to say your name more often than usual.

Building Positive Self-Esteem: The Secret? If you ask people what they want out of life, the four most common responses include: happiness; feeling good about yourself; health; and productivity. Consider "feeling good about yourself," also known as self-esteem. To a large extent, this is defined as the strength of belief you have in yourself to be needed, important, recognized, and appreciated for your societal contributions. *Accordingly, having a positive self-esteem leads to a happier, more energetic, highly productive life—the gateway to success.* Perhaps the significance of this relation was best expressed by former Vice President Joe Biden when he enthusiastically whispered to President Obama, "This is a big f-bomb deal" over an open microphone. (See Figure 11.1.)

So, if attaining and maintaining positive self-esteem is highly advantageous in life, how does one achieve it? Where does self-esteem come from? Although many people feel it emanates from themselves, internally, behavioral scientists tell us it doesn't work that way. The reason is that we largely get our self-esteem, our picture of ourselves, from the way others respond to us. In fact, we are dependent on other people's interactions with us to build our self-esteem. Unfortunately, the tendency for those with negative self-esteem, up to 77 percent of the population at any given time, is to drag us down. So, what can we do?

According to one authority on self-esteem, Steven A. Goren, PhD, the answer lies in our ability to keep our attitudes positive and find ways of building the self-esteem of others around us. How do you do that? Make your compliments and acknowledgments SPECIFIC. "Susan, congratulations on the letter I received from one of our grateful patients regarding the wonderful experience he had in our program. You were

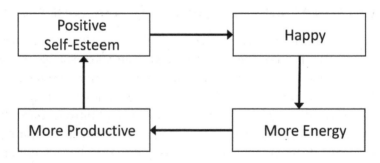

FIGURE 11.1
Positive self-esteem leads to a happier, more energetic, highly productive life——the gateway to success.

specifically mentioned, numerous times! I plan to read it aloud at our staff meeting tomorrow." Don't just say, "Susan, you do a great job for us." If you can learn to build up your colleagues and support staff, make them feel good about themselves, and put them into that positive frame of mind, they'll likely do the same for you. Why? Because people generally respond in kind. Build the confidence and self-esteem of those around you and you'll find the secret to a happy, energetic, and productive life.

Let People Know That You Appreciate Them. A masterful paperback book entitled *A Touch of Wonder*, by Arthur Gordon, highlighted an "Achilles heel" that applies to so many of us—people don't often take the opportunity to share with family, friends, students, and colleagues their heartfelt sentiments about them. These are the people that love us, admire us, and help us in so many different ways. Accordingly, years ago, I got in the habit of putting people I strongly supported on blind copy of recommendations, nominations, and letters/emails I sent on their behalf. I wanted them to know what I thought of their great qualities. Moreover, if they ended up not getting the job, promotion, or award, at least they knew I had their back. Because of my sharing with them my positive sentiments about them, many have generously reciprocated through their support of my goals and aspirations.

There is a woefully underused phrase that, when sincerely stated, can provide a small token of our appreciation and gratitude. "Have I told you lately what a wonderful person you are?" The significance of these words, from you, to the people that regularly lift you up, will lift them up. When was the last time you said them?

CELEBRATING STAFF BIRTHDAYS: A GREAT IDEA!

A wonderful gift is sharing kind words, compliments, accomplishments, and traits of others you admire. To celebrate staff birthdays, we adopted the practice of asking all staff to make a list of the nicest things (ideally in one to five words) about each of their co-workers that could be shared, anonymously, on a staff member's birthday. One staff member spearheads the tributes, on a rotating basis, assimilating the comments on a standard letter-size birthday card, which is presented to the recipient with everyone in attendance. These cards always generate a ton of laughter and smiles, let people know how much they are appreciated, and are a wonderful morale booster. I've always considered my cards as "keepers," which I invariably pull out when I'm having a bad day.

During the long, often dangerously boring drive from Phoenix Arizona to Las Vegas Nevada, there are posted signs along the endless road, at sites of horrific, deadly accidents, warning drivers not to drive if they've been drinking alcohol and/or are sleep deprived. The signs say:

THERE IS A LAST TIME FOR EVERYTHING.

Take a few minutes *today* to say or write something nice to or about a family member, friend, or colleague. Why? Because they (or you) might be gone tomorrow. There is a last time for everything.

You cannot do a kindness too soon because you never know when it will be too late.

Ralph Waldo Emerson

12

Be Willing to Pay the Price: The Law of Sow and Reap

"None of the secrets of success will work unless you do." Many years ago, I found this fortune inside a cookie at a Chinese restaurant—and decided to keep it. The fact of the matter is that you will not be successful by simply reading this book or attending my class or presentation on the topic. You've got to integrate these success principles and skills you learn into your life and practice them on a daily basis. The analogy is trying to improve your foul shots, tennis, or golf game from simply reading a book or having a private lesson without applying what you learned in real life. *Hard work remains an integral forerunner of future success.*

Consider the following quotes when gauging the role of "hard work" as a key strategy for future success:

> If people only knew how hard I worked to gain mastery, it wouldn't seem wonderful at all.
>
> **Michelangelo**

> Hard work beats talent when talent fails to work hard.
> **Professional basketball player Kevin Durant**

> The only place where *success* comes before *work* is in the dictionary.
> **British hairstylist Vidal Sassoon**

> Hard work does not necessarily guarantee success, but no success is possible without hard work.
> **Former political prisoner Dr. T.P. Chia**

DOI: 10.4324/9781003260387-14

The only thing that ever sat on its way to success was a hen.
Emmy-winning actress Sarah Brown

You can't hire someone else to do your push-ups for you.
Entrepreneur, author, motivational speaker Jim Rohn

HARD WORK VERSUS TALENT AS REQUISITES FOR SUCCESS?

In the real world, innate talent is a commodity. But it is hard work that differentiates the chumps from the champions. In his recent book *Peak*, Professor Anders Ericsson at Florida State University dispels the myth that success comes just from pure talent. His conclusion: "If you don't try hard, no matter how much talent you have, there's always going to be someone else who has a similar amount of talent who outworks you, and therefore outperforms you." There are countless examples of highly successful people with legendary work ethics across all disciplines.

Consider that at 6 years of age, Tiger Woods listened to motivational tapes while practicing his golf swing in the mirror. The late Kobe Bryant became one of the NBA's superstars by starting practice 3 hours earlier than his teammates, even when he was injured with a cast on his wrist. Mozart achieved success not because he was born with talent, but because his father trained him to be a concert pianist and composer from the age of four. Elvis Presley cultivated his singing and entertainment skills by performing shows almost daily—doing 315 shows in 1955, sometimes being featured in two or three shows on the same day! In business, Gary Vaynerchuk (Vayner Media), Marissa Mayer (chief executive officer at Yahoo), and Elon Musk (Tesla and Space X) all report working 80 to 130 hours per week. Although excessive work commitments like these have been linked with poor health and high stress, what critics fail to realize is that these top performers *love their work*. Knowing their frenetic schedules, they also work more efficiently than most people, prioritizing their "to do" lists, delegating time-consuming tasks to others, and strategically re-energizing by combining business and pleasure trips. Overall, the daily grind appears to be outweighed by the euphoria conferred by regularly attaining their lofty goals and aspirations.

The following quotes, stories, and testimonials highlight the impact of hard work and practice, practice, practice as a harbinger of overwhelming success in professional sports and music, which are further substantiated by the 10,000-hour rule.

Jack Nicklaus (professional golfer) had a great effect on my career—more than he'll ever know. I realized early on, that if I was going to compete with him, I'd have to practice harder than he did.

Lee Trevino

Steve Alford, NBA player and Olympic gold medalist, was once interviewed about his Olympic experience. He said:

When I played with Michael Jordan on the Olympic team, there was a huge gap between his ability and the ability of other great players on the team. But what impressed me was that he (Michael) was always the first one on the floor and the last one to leave.

Similarly, legendary basketball coach Rick Pitino, commenting on Michael Jordan, said:

He practices harder than anyone on the court—and expects to be successful because he has *paid the price* to be successful.

Golfing legend Gary Player, who is now in his 80s and still playing some professional golf, was walking through an airport one day, and a guy looked at him and said, "Aren't you Gary Player, the famous golfer from South Africa?" Player replied, "Yes, I'm Gary Player." The guy said, "Wow! I've been watching you on TV for years. You're unbelievable. You know, I'd do anything to hit a golf ball like you." And Player, who's normally a diplomat, responded:

You'd do anything to hit a golf ball like me if you didn't have to practice. You know what you got to do to hit a golf ball like me? You've got to get up at 4:30 am every day, go hit hundreds of golf balls till your hands are swollen and tender, go back to the club house, ice your hands, get a cup of coffee and a piece of toast or muffin, go back and hit another 1,000 balls, and then go out and play 18, 27, or 36 holes. You'd do anything to hit a golf ball like me if you didn't have to practice.

I love the related account that leadership guru John C. Maxwell shares. Sarasate, the greatest Spanish violinist of the 19th century, was once called a genius by a famous critic. In reply to this, Sarasate said, "Genius! For 37 years I've practiced 14 hours a day, and now they call me a genius."

Similarly, the story of Fritz Kreisler, the great violinist, beautifully illustrates the relation between passion, hard work, discipline, and overwhelming success. After a virtuoso performance, he was approached by a woman who said, "Mr. Kreisler, I would give my life to play as you have!" He smiled at the woman and replied, "I did!"

PREPARING FOR SUCCESS

The great Italian violinist Niccolō Paganini was once partway through a solo performance when one of his strings suddenly broke—then a second string snapped, and then a third, leaving him with only a single violin string. He not only continued but flawlessly carried off a virtuoso performance, even limited to a single string, as the audience watched in awe! How did he do it? He had put in long hours practicing the instrument without all its strings, and even composed music to be played on a violin with just one string.

When recounting this particular story, Professor Ericsson commented: "Achievement takes preparation. Once you understand what an individual actually did to prepare for these kinds of events, then it becomes more understandable."

In his book *Outliers*, Malcolm Gladwell shares his "10,000 Hour Rule" as a common trait of highly successful people. To really be good at something, Gladwell emphasizes that you've got to devote more than 10,000 hours to it. That's 20 hours per week for 10 years! He goes on to discuss professional athletes, tech-savvy businessmen like Bill Gates, and musicians like the Beatles, who tallied over 1,200 live performances from 1960 to 1964, amassing greater than 10,000 hours of practice/playing time. They all prepared for their success. Consider the saga of Bill Gates. At 13 years of age, his father, a highly successful lawyer in Seattle, sent him to a private school that had one of the only computers in the United States where students could do real-time programming. Two years later, Gates learned there was a giant mainframe computer at the nearby University of Washington that was not being used between 2:00 am and 6:00 am. So, Bill would set his alarm for 1:30 am, walk a mile, and program for 4 hours. During the course of 7 months, he accumulated ~1,600 hours of computer time, and by the time he dropped out of Harvard after his sophomore year to establish his own computer software company, he had been programming nonstop for seven consecutive years. Through this accelerated practice plan, he had accumulated way more than 10,000 hours! The moral of the story? *Success doesn't happen by chance.*

So, I tell my students:

> No, you're probably not going to be a great writer or a great speaker at this stage of the game, but devote your time and effort, and take every opportunity to write, speak, and improve your computer skills. You will be there someday. But first, you've got to accumulate those 10,000+ hours. Prepare, prepare, prepare, prepare. *Pay the price*! Even when I give this presentation on success secrets—a presentation that I've now given hundreds of times, I practice. I practice in the evening … I wake up early and go through it again, several more times, before actually giving the talk that day. The bottom line? People who do things well have put countless hours practicing it over the years. You're no exception. You, too, have got to *pay the price*. Start today—accumulating those hours—a great investment in your future!

The "losers in life" will often stand by, observing the most successful among us, and remark, "I wish I had her talent!" or "I wish I had his luck," with no conception of the years of disciplined effort (and sacrifice) that molded that person's performance. How often do we read about the "overnight success" in show business and find that this new superstar has been slogging away (with countless setbacks and rejections) for many years, and sometimes decades?

CULTURE AND ACHIEVEMENT

Do the roots of ambition lie in genes, family, education, culture, economic class, or primarily in your own hands? The greatest proportion of ambitious people appear to come from the upper middle class. Researchers have also reported that two of the biggest influences on people's level of ambition are the family that produced them and the culture behind the family. Gladwell further emphasized that culture is an important modulator of success. He contends that the culture we belong to and the legacies passed down by our parents and grandparents (e.g., importance of education, work ethic) shape the patterns and magnitude of our achievements in astonishing ways. For example, Gladwell highlights the fact that many modern-day math geniuses are Asians. The link, he contends, may be related, at least in part, to the hard work, patience, and dedication that stems from the cultivation of growing rice. An additional reinforcer, he notes, is that cultures that embrace education, training, and a tireless work ethic don't give their children extended summer vacations. Consider the school year for Japan, South Korea, and the United States, at 243, 220, and 180 days, respectively.

THE LAW OF SOW AND REAP

Success is simply a matter of luck. Ask any failure!

American journalist, author Earl Wilson

Striving for success without hard work is like trying to harvest where you haven't planted.

Retired teacher and politician David Bly

Don't be like the person sitting in front of that empty fireplace and asking for heat; you're asking for the impossible. Pile the wood in first. The heat will come as a result.

Earl Nightingale

What you do today can improve all your tomorrows."

Personal development guru Ralph Marston

Don't judge each day by the harvest you reap, but by the seeds you plant.

Robert Louis Stevenson

Newton discovered the law of cause and effect, that is, for every action there is an equal and opposite reaction. How does this law impact your life? It functions like a boomerang. You throw it out, and it comes back to you. *But we only get back something if we first act.* And if we plant tomatoes, we reap tomatoes, not onions. Recognize that this "principle of specificity" affects virtually everything we do and every reciprocal event we experience in life. For example, if we treat people nicely or poorly, via the law of cause and effect, we'll likely be treated by them in a similar manner. Our physical and mental health, business or academic success, and personal relationships are each governed by the same law, which requires us to "pay up front." The "good news" about the law is that we never know when we will be rewarded, and the rewards are invariably much greater than our investment.

This introduction leads us to "the law of sow and reap." To reap is to "gather a crop," and to sow is "to plant seeds." Sowing is used as a metaphor for one's actions and reaping for harvesting the results of those actions. In other words, future outcomes are inevitably shaped by present actions, or, what you do today can influence all your tomorrows. Do we always reap what we sow? Yes, the universal and immutable law of cause and effect orchestrates the outcome. However, if you wish to reap, you must sow. Accordingly, what you have in your life today is a result of the sowing that you have done until now. If your business is currently flourishing, it is because you've already expended the effort (i.e., planting the seeds) to justify the dividends you're receiving.

Every farmer understands the significance of this law: We reap what we sow, but always more than we sow, and at a later date. This principle applies to everyone (believers and non-believers), is irrevocable, and is a law of life. *Essentially, you ultimately receive more than you put in.* Accordingly, it is the shortsighted person who thinks only of the now, doing as little as possible in the present, for on payday he/she will have no way to avoid the meager rewards for their efforts.

As a child, I remember an elementary school teacher explaining to the class about the importance of saving money, investing it wisely, and that even more money (via compound interest) would accumulate over time, making us wealthy when we're older. The law of sowing and reaping has many similarities. For example, farmers have come to expect to harvest a great deal more than they sow. Why? Because the wonderful thing about nature is that it gives us back much more than we put out. Plant a few pumpkin seeds, till and nurture the soil over time, and you may end up with a truckload of pumpkins containing thousands of seeds.

It's the same way in life—positive actions today, like getting additional training or education, sending a "thank you" note, providing a needed service or product for customers, or simply treating people the way you'd want to be treated, will produce a rich harvest in the future. On the other hand, if we tell lies or rip people off, we can expect to be lied to or ripped off in the future. To reiterate, this principle applies to everything we do, but first we need to get out in the fields and plant the seeds!

In summary, I sincerely believe that every person is born to be accomplished at something they enjoy doing and are good at. The purpose of his or her life is to discover it and then spend years cultivating whatever plot of ground they were given to sow, till, and reap (the rewards). As previously stated, focus on your contributions and service to others, and the rewards will come. My take home message? The universe is fair and just. To a large extent, you get back from life what *you* put into it—and more. Sow now, reap later. What you plant must come back. Plant only good thoughts. Stop planting "negative" seeds or things you fear. And remember: the magnitude of the rewards or reaping that you desire should be in concert with the depth and breadth of your actions and contributions (sowing). If you follow this advice, nothing can stop you from ultimately acquiring what you desire.

FORGET ABOUT GOING "THE EXTRA MILE" ONCE OR TWICE A YEAR: GO THE EXTRA INCH IN EVERYTHING YOU DO!

Josh Linkner, a tech entrepreneur, best-selling author, and success guru, described a seated audience who were asked to raise their hands as high as they could. Then, the speaker asked them to raise their hands an extra inch. Virtually all accomplished this feat, with no major complications or injuries. Linkner contends, and I believe he is right, that if we go the extra inch in everything we do, that little bit of extra effort in every deliverable you may produce will, over time, make you a winner in life! And, in contrast to going the extra mile, recognize that you have a nearly limitless supply of stretching that additional inch in everything you do. His concluding message? "Give generously."

OVERCOMING INERTIA: "THE MASTER WORD"

In closing this chapter, it's only when we start the job and begin to *work* at it that we find we have the power and talent to make our desire a reality.

As long as we sit and merely ponder it, wish for it, and take no action to overcome inertia, we will never gain the momentum we need to make it happen. I ran across an infallible strategy that applies to all of us in overcoming inertia—the single greatest barrier to success. It's a word that will *work* wonders for a person regardless of their age or what they do during their lifetime. In essence, it's magnificently captured in the following quote by the great physician Sir William Osler:

> Though little, the master word looms large in meaning. It is the "open sesame" to every portal, the great equalizer, the philosopher's stone which transmutes all base metal of humanity into gold. The stupid it will make bright, the bright brilliant, and the brilliant steady. To youth it brings hope, to the middle-aged confidence, to the aged repose.

Do you know what the master word is? Guess. I used it twice in the paragraph preceding Osler's quote. Did you recognize it?

Well—the master word is—WORK! *Pay the price.*

Talk is not a substitute for action—but work is.

Section III

Additional Strategies and Tactics for Success

13

Be Driven: Don't Leave
Any Stone Unturned

In addition to the aforementioned foundational factors, behavioral skills, strategies and secrets for success, complementary approaches, tactics, and perspectives can help you achieve the life that you've imagined. These include: time management and the 80/20 rule; looking for greener pastures; showcasing your talents (visibility → opportunities); committing to never-ending improvement; embracing discipline/focus to pursue your goals; routinely exceeding people's expectations; striving for greater rewards (i.e., going for the "gold" in everything you do); and seeing an ocean of opportunities before you.

TIME MANAGEMENT: APPLYING THE 80/20 RULE TO ACCOMPLISH MORE

It has been my observation that most people get ahead during the time that others waste.

Henry Ford

Time is precious—the great equalizer. We all start the day with the same 24 hours. Our success depends heavily on how well we use this resource. Why? Because once it's gone, whether invested wisely or squandered foolishly, it can never be recaptured. I've witnessed a common denominator in carefully observing highly successful, incredibly productive people over the years, that is, their focus in pulling together potentially wasted

DOI: 10.4324/9781003260387-16

seconds, minutes, and hours (for others) to accomplish what they want to in their transit and free time (e.g., during cab rides, waiting for and during flights). My most memorable observation? Walking into a men's restroom at the convention center during a major annual sports medicine conference and seeing one of the most prolific scientists I know, writing on a sheet of paper he was holding on the wall, as he stood at the urinal. "Roy, what could you possibly be working on?" I asked. "It's for a research report I'm writing," he matter-of-factly replied.

Highly successful people use small periods of time, throughout the day, every day, to accomplish big jobs. They've also discovered other ways to find additional time each day by turning off the television and learning to say "no" to projects, unrealistic deadlines, and invitations that do not truly serve their goals. Moreover, they've stopped surfing the internet, running non-essential errands, and being available (and interrupted) 24/7 via calls, text messages, and emails. Many of these communications are irrelevant, unrelated to their job, or other people's queries that can wait. They've learned to respond, en masse, later in the day, at their convenience. Empiric experience and proven time-saving tips include: avoiding checking emails in the morning; replying to emails by fitting the entire response on one line (some people waste hours each day crafting long, detailed responses); answering the phone with "How can I be of assistance?" rather than, "How are you?" which is an invitation to chat; focusing on a single job during a specific time frame, rather than multi-tasking, which leads to inefficient work practices; and, when someone approaches you for advice, responding with "How much time do you need?" If it's more than a few seconds, ask them to schedule an appointment. In the interim, the person often solves the problem on their own.

TIME MANAGEMENT: THE SECRET?

There's an old saying that goes, "If you want something done quickly, give it to an individual who is way too busy to do it. They'll find time for it." What have they learned that you haven't? Beat procrastination and indecision, and you'll start finding time for more things than you ever imagined. How? Start the job. If you simply take the first step in any direction, your "action" will build momentum, and the job will get done!

Achieving more with less—the 80/20 rule. Successful people also increasingly focus on and develop their core genius (i.e., what they love to do and do very well, better than their competitors)—and delegate other routine tasks to a talented support team. To enhance and refine these core competencies, they abandon what isn't working, embrace ongoing self-reflection, identify future opportunities, and learn how to bring them to fruition. Based on empiric experience and numerous supporting analyses, they've come to the sobering realization that about 20 percent of their activities generate about 80 percent of their most rewarding successes. This revelation, about inequality, is referred to as the Pareto Principle, which was originally named after Vilfredo Pareto—an Italian economist who in 1895 found that about 80 percent of Italy's land belonged to 20 percent of the country's (wealthiest) population. Subsequent studies in a variety of fields (e.g., taxation, project management, business, medicine, information technology) have shown that most of the time, related comparisons are distributed unevenly. From a practical perspective, what does that mean for you? To maximize efficiency and productivity, relative to time management, you should identify and focus even more time on the vital 20 percent of activities that yield approximately 80 percent of your most rewarding achievements (see Figure 13.1).

In summary, the 80/20 rule is one of the great secrets of highly effective people, organizations, and businesses. The rule isn't as much a scientific theory as an observation that things are distributed unequally most of the

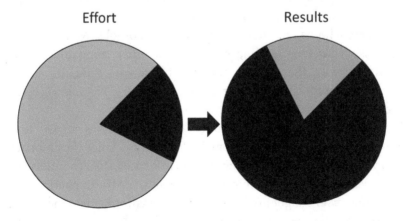

FIGURE 13.1
The Pareto Principle: Approximately 20 percent of your daily activities yield about 80 percent of your most rewarding achievements.

time. It's based on the repeated finding that approximately 80 percent of all our important outcomes or results in business and in life stem from a mere 20 percent of our efforts. The unspoken corollary of the Pareto Principle is that little of what we spend our time on actually pays big dividends. By focusing more on those activities that do, we can unlock the enormous potential of the outcome-driven 20 percent and supercharge our effectiveness in our jobs, our careers, our businesses, and our lives.

LOOKING FOR GREENER PASTURES? PROCEED WITH CAUTION

According to an Economic News release from the Bureau of Labor Statistics, the average duration that wage and salary employees have worked for their current employer is 4.6 years. Lots of moving around—in large part, looking for greener pastures. Indeed, job hopping has become increasingly popular. Promotion, leadership opportunities, gaining new knowledge, skills, and abilities, professional advancement, and salary increases are commonly cited reasons. However, people who frequently change jobs often lose months in adapting to learning curves and demographic and corporate transitions and are cautiously viewed by companies that value loyalty. On the other hand, staying too long with the same company, especially without being promoted, can be a red flag to a potential employer, suggesting a less diverse and evolved set of skills than a candidate who has mastered a broader range of jobs. Many employers might also view longstanding employees at other companies as being comfortable with the familiar and possibly having difficulty adapting to a new job, leadership style, or corporate culture. Notable exceptions, however, include academics and medicine.

A relevant story, "Acres of Diamonds," made famous by Dr. Russell Herman Conwell, who founded Temple University, detailed the unfortunate journey of a farmer who sold his homestead in Africa to join countless others in their search for diamond mines throughout the African continent. One day, the man who bought his farm, crossing a small stream on the property, found a large glimmering stone on the creek's bottom. He believed it was crystal and placed it on his fireplace mantel as a curio. Subsequently, a visitor to his home nearly fainted when he saw it and confirmed that he'd picked up one of the largest diamonds ever found! The owner revealed that the creek was loaded with such stones, most not as large as the one on the mantel. Accordingly, the farm that the first farmer sold to allow him to prospect for diamonds elsewhere proved to be the most productive diamond mine on the entire African continent. And, the first farmer? He died penniless and despondent after years of futile searching.

The moral is clear: We should carefully examine the job opportunities we have in hand before we run off to perceived greener pastures, as there may be "acres of diamonds" at our feet if we simply look for them.

SHOWCASING YOUR TALENTS: VISIBILITY → OPPORTUNITIES

You can have all the talent in the world, but if you don't have visibility—if people don't know about you—you'll have few or no opportunities and limited success. As I view the most successful and talented people in the world, they get plenty of exposure ... as they have the *Visibility Factor.* Get outside your immediate environment! Join national associations, clubs, committees ... publish ... speak ... seek media interviews (radio, television, newspapers), use social media ... take every opportunity you can to showcase yourself, your business, and the services you provide. Over time, strive to get on the annual programs as a presenter at major business or association meetings with thousands of attendees. *If I've learned anything about success, it's that visibility leads to opportunities.*

In any field of endeavor—in every field of endeavor—the leaders are promoters. If you are the company/department president, chief executive officer, director, or manager, take action! You should be regularly outside your office—promoting your ideas, your staff, your service line, your products, and your business. An added bonus is that in doing so, you are also promoting yourself. I call this the "Visibility Threshold." Your future opportunities are directly linked with your visibility and exponentially increase once you start getting on the internet, social media, newspapers, radio, and television. Why? Because when your visibility goes from tens, to hundreds, to thousands, to millions of people who see you, hear you, or read about you or what you have written, a percentage of these individuals are going to want to recruit YOU for a talk, consulting,

Take *Action* To Promote Yourself, Your Ideas, Your Staff, Your Service Line, Products and Business

> In EVERY field of endeavor, in ANY field of endeavor, the leaders are promoters.

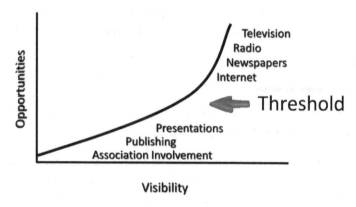

FIGURE 13.2

authorship, media interviews, or other forms of collaboration—leading to additional visibility. To me, increased visibility is a magnet for future opportunities and success, as I've consistently experienced it in my own career. I've learned that in many respects, seeing, hearing, or reading your perspectives is a form of sowing. And, the rewards are proportionate to the size of your audience. Sow now, reap later (see Figure 13.2).

Finally, recognize that many people have become overwhelmingly successful simply by making themselves available. You've got to be there when the opportunity arises. Persistence pays! Remember that setbacks or rejections (temporary "no's"), repeated over time, may ultimately lead to success (e.g., the client you visited 12 times before you got the big order). This represents another variation in the "visibility leads to opportunities" theme.

COMMIT TO NEVER-ENDING IMPROVEMENT

This point is critically important—one of the most enlightening lessons that I'll share with you in this entire book! Any time a student or young professional says to me, "I'm thinking about getting a Master's degree, obtaining certification to validate my knowledge, skills, and abilities in my chosen field, or taking an additional course to strengthen my competency," I always say, "Go for it! Make yourself a little bit better." The Professional Golfers' Association (PGA) is a microcosm of the real world. Annual PGA rankings are particularly insightful when comparing good with great people in any field. Let me show you what I mean.

Back in 2002, I started compiling the average PGA tour scores for each round of golf (18 holes) for the "top 10" golfers each year. That year, Tiger Woods was the #1 golfer in the world. For each round of golf in the PGA tour, he averaged 68.56 strokes. The #10 golfer in the world that year, Sergio Garcia, averaged 70.0 strokes per 18 holes. What does that mean? Every time they played, Tiger Woods would beat Sergio Garcia by, on average, a stroke and a half. Specifically, 1.44 shots! (Subsequent years showed similar differences between the #1 and #10 golfers each year, approximating 2 or fewer shots per 18 holes.) In 2002, Tiger Woods won $6.9 million; Sergio Garcia, $2.4 million. Neither one had a bad payday.

That same year, Nike decided to give a lucrative marketing contract to the top golfer in the world—a multimillion-dollar deal. Who got it? Tiger Woods—because he could beat the second-place finisher, Vijay Singh, by 0.91 shots and the tenth-place finisher, Sergio Garcia, by 1.44 shots, per 18 holes of golf! What's the moral of the story? Don't rest on your laurels. Constantly try to make yourself (or your performance) a little bit better. Small improvements in life yield BIG rewards (see Figure 13.3).

The Small Difference Between Stardom and Mediocrity. The gap between huge success and mediocrity, in sports and in life, is seldom very wide. Major league baseball provides another sobering example. A professional baseball player who hits .320 may make $5 million a year, whereas a member of the same team who hits .220 might be paid $500,000. All the .220 hitter must do to increase his salary 10-fold is to average 1 more hit for each 10 at bats. In essence, to be considered a "star," he must slightly increase his ratio of hits to strike, ground, or fly outs. *But, he's got to start thinking beyond conventional practices and game play to improve his performance—which isn't getting him to his highly paid teammate's batting average.* Perhaps extra time in the batting cage and/or a training regimen to improve muscular strength, running speed, and reaction time, or combinations thereof, will do the trick? Offseason play coupled

It Pays to be Just
a Little Bit Better:

PGA Tour 2002 Scoring Average

Rank	Player	Average
1	Tiger Woods*	68.56
2	Vijay Singh	69.47
3	Ernie Els	69.50
4	Phil Mickelson	69.58
5	Nick Price	69.59
6	Retief Goosen	69.69
7	David Toms	69.73
8	Justin Leonard	69.86
9	Fred Funk	69.99
10	Sergio Garcia**	70.00

* $6.9 million; ** $2.4 million

FIGURE 13.3

with continued physical conditioning is an additional option. These adjunctive improvement strategies alone may also reframe his mindset (i.e., constantly thinking about becoming a better hitter) to enhance his batting average.

If your success ratio is 50 percent right now, increasing it to even 60 percent would likely make an enormous difference in your performance (and pay), regardless of your field. Make a concerted effort to learn from each failure or setback, develop a multifaceted plan to rectify your deficiencies, and aggressively pursue the plan. With this approach, you'll be well on your way to stardom.

> Your goal isn't to be better than anyone else. Your goal is to be better than you used to be.
>
> **Motivational guru Dr. Wayne W. Dyer**

And if you adopt this approach, some day you may, in fact, be better than anyone else. ☺

USE DISCIPLINE TO RELENTLESSLY PURSUE YOUR GOALS

Discipline is the bridge between goals and achievement.

Jim Rohn

Discipline is to your life's success what carbon is to steel: You need the one to have the other. The ability to give yourself a directive and follow it is imperative in order to achieve the life of your dreams. I was a gymnast in college, and so national class gymnasts were, of course, among those I studied for success secrets. When Olympic gymnast Peter Vidmar was asked, "How'd you become a Gold Medalist?" he replied. "To be a champion, I had to do two things: Work out when I wanted to and work out when I didn't." It's as simple as that. That's called discipline or focus. And, needless to say, its counterpart is sacrifice—in order to achieve a breakthrough life goal or aspiration. *Success doesn't happen by chance.*

ROUTINELY EXCEED PEOPLE'S EXPECTATIONS

In his small but powerful best-seller *The Fred Factor*, an internationally known author, motivational speaker, and leadership consultant, Mark Sanborn (who was kind enough to write the Foreword for this book), recounts the true story of Fred, his mail carrier, a man who passionately loves his occupation and who genuinely cares about the people he serves. Because of that, he is constantly going the extra mile in handling the mail, watching over the houses and people on his route, and treating everyone he meets as a friend—with dignity and respect.

There are four basic principles that define *The Fred Factor*. First, regardless of your job title, nobody can prevent you from choosing to be exceptional. In other words, there are no unimportant jobs, just people who feel inconsequential doing their jobs. Second, service becomes personalized when a relationship exists between the provider and the customer. Third, Freds have the ability to create value for customers without doling out to do it. Finally, you can make your lifework, as well as your life, anything you choose it to be. In essence, *The Fred Factor* provides a poignant parable of success. *It's about routinely exceeding your clients/customers' expectations.*

Successful people and businesses routinely exceed people's expectations. Let me share with you three relevant stories, the latter two of which are personal.

Manhattan cabbie. I read this brief story several years ago and found it particularly insightful. It was about a cab driver who makes $40,000+ a year more in tips than any other cabbie in Manhattan. Why? He offers passengers a choice of music, newspapers, hot coffee, bottled water, and exemplary service. You can even choose the radio station or type of music you want to listen to! You enter his spotless, smoke-free cab, and right away it's a "Wow moment," and the driver asks, "Would you like a copy of the *USA Today* or the *Wall Street Journal*?" He spends money in advance on his customers, but gets it all back and more, by exceeding their expectations. You'd be embarrassed not to leave a generous tip. In hectic, brusque Manhattan, his unique approach in routinely exceeding his customers' expectations makes him stand out.

My Beaumont contract. I was recruited in 1985 to apply for a position opening at Beaumont Hospital, Royal Oak, Michigan. The co-directors of the department of cardiology at the time, Drs. Seymour Gordon and Gerald Timmis, invited me to interview one evening in a dark pub, where I was asked numerous questions—including the salary that it would take to move me to Beaumont. I stated a figure and they replied, "We may be able to do that." However, they mentioned that I'd have to interview with additional hospital and medical administrators, including Dr. Rutzky, the chief medical officer, before a contract could be offered.

I completed the remaining interviews, including one with Dr. Rutzky, which required me to submit a detailed written proposal on my vision for the future of preventive cardiology/rehabilitation, as well as my specific job responsibilities. I was subsequently contacted, informed that I had been selected for the position, and that I would need to go to Dr. Rutzky's office the next day to review and sign my contract. As I was carefully reading the contract in a corner of Dr. Rutzky's office, I found an error and promptly brought this to his attention. He said, "What's the error?" I replied, "The salary is $5,000 more than we agreed to." He looked at me rather intimidatingly and barked, "You don't determine the salary. I do. And, you're worth $5,000 more than the salary we discussed." Needless to say, that unexpected surprise got my attention … and exceeding my expectations strongly motivated me to do the same. I came to the realization that Dr. Rutzky was a pretty smart guy. He also understood a key tenet of human behavior, that is, if you exceed people's expectations, they'll generally respond in kind. I certainly did—working countless extra hours and often weekends to show him that his confidence in me and the starting salary were justified.

My Northwest Airlines story. In the mid-1990s, I had the good fortune of working on a national *Cardiac Rehabilitation Clinical Practice Guideline* with a team of experts, including a superb writer, Joseph Piscatella, who at 32 years of age had undergone triple vessel coronary artery bypass surgery. Joe had written a couple of best-selling books on heart health, so when he subsequently asked, "Barry, would you co-author my next book with me?" I couldn't say no! Long story short, we had just written *Take a Load off Your Heart*, and I was flying a lot at the time. One day, I was sitting in business class, getting ready to take off on a Northwest flight. Just as they're closing the door to the plane, a tall athletic looking guy, big shoulders, small waist, well-dressed, came in and sat next to me. He looked like a professional football player. I saw a huge ring on his finger, which made me think, "Am I sitting next to a Super Bowl player, and I don't know who the hell this is?" So, I said, "Geez, you look very familiar. Are you a professional athlete?" He started laughing at me and said, "No, I used to play amateur hockey in Canada." I said, "Well, what do you do now?" He replied, "I'm the vice president of Northwest Airlines." He asked me, "What do you do?" I said, "I just direct a cardiac rehab program at William Beaumont Hospital." He went on, "You know, my dad just had a heart attack about a month ago, and he's trying to learn about cholesterol and how to improve his heart health." I happened to have a copy of our just-published book in my briefcase. Without thinking twice, I opened it up and gave the book to him. I said, "Give this to your dad." He replied, "How much do I owe you?" I said, "You don't owe me anything. I hope it's helpful to your dad." He said, "Thanks very much, Dr. Franklin, I really appreciate it." (By the way, that book cost me about $6.00 because I pay half the cover price.)

As we were flying, he asked me, "Dr. Franklin, what do you think of Northwest Airlines?" I said, "I think you guys are great. I fly you all the time, but I just have one complaint." He asked, "What's that?" I replied, "Whenever I fly international, which is one or two times a year, I try to use my Frequent Flyer miles to upgrade to Business Class, but there's never a seat." He started laughing again. I asked, "What are you laughing at now?" He said, "There's almost always a seat." I responded, "Not when Barry Franklin calls the Northwest help-line." He paused for a second and reached into his pocket, "Here's my card. My name's Jeff. You were nice enough to give me a copy of your new book for my dad. Call me in the future when you want to be upgraded; we'll apply your Frequent Flyer mileage for a seat in Business Class." I used him for five or six international trips. It was great. Indeed, I was sorry to see Northwest get bought out by Delta. But for a $6.00 book, look what it did for me. Priceless! Now, whenever I sit next to somebody on a plane, I never hesitate to try to start up a conversation. Why? Because you never know who you might be sitting next to—and as I previously stated, you can't know too many people.

STRIVE FOR GREATER REWARDS

A high school teacher said to his graduating class, "I know a lot of you are going to college next year. I also know you know this material, so for those of you who want to skip the final, I'll give you an automatic 'B' on the exam." Most everybody said, "Whoa! That's great," because the final would have taken them 2 hours to complete. Nearly all of the students walked out, thanking the teacher profusely. But four students remained. The teacher said, "Well, guess you remaining students want to take the final, then, right?" They replied, "Yeah." One student remarked, "I studied really hard for this exam, and believe I can do better than a B." Then the teacher proceeded to pass out a one-page final exam. It said, "Congratulations! You've just received an 'A' in this class. Keep believing in yourself." I tell our students, staff, and younger colleagues: "Don't settle for the 'B.' Go for the gold in everything you do in life."

SEE AN OCEAN OF OPPORTUNITIES

Foster Hibbard tells the story of two men who walk down to the ocean, one with a teaspoon, the other with a bucket, each taking away the amount of water he chose to withdraw. In so many ways, the ocean represents the opportunities and associated rewards you have in life. It represents abundance, and abundance doesn't care if you come down to it with a teaspoon, bucket, or tanker truck—as it is a miraculously replenishing, unlimited resource. Your withdrawals (e.g., clients serviced, sales commissions, publications, trips taken, paid consulting invitations) don't diminish anyone else's opportunities, nor do their accomplishments diminish the total amount of abundance available to you. It is infinite!

Don't waste your time and effort focused on your competitor's successes and accomplishments (i.e., how much water they withdraw from the ocean). Why? Because it transiently forces you to take your eye off the ball and diverts your attention from your goals and aspirations. Moreover, their withdrawals have no impact on your share of the ocean. *One of life's great success secrets can be summarized in just three words: "Compete with yourself."* Forget what others are or are not doing. Don't compete with them! Try to sell more this month than you sold last month, or if you are a funded researcher, try to increase the quantity and quality of your grant proposals this year as compared with last year.

> Your goal isn't to be better than anyone else. Your goal is to be better than you used to be.
> **Motivational guru Dr. Wayne W. Dyer**

I decided, long ago, that when I approached the ocean, it was going to be with a damn tanker truck. I filled that sucker up and have been back to the shore (for refills) on numerous occasions. Your opportunities and rewards are limited only by your vision of what you want in life. Your accomplishments and rewards don't compromise anyone else's, and vice versa. Whatever you are willing to accept is what you get. We get what we expect (and are willing to accept) from life. If you expect more, and plunge in (to that ocean) after it, you'll get it. The only limits on your share are placed there by you.

If you want more, you have to require more from yourself.

Dr. Phil

14

Be a Finisher: Final Thoughts on Aligning Yourself with Destiny and Good Fortune

In the current era of information access and exchange, professors (like myself) are sometimes asked, often near the end of their careers, to give lectures on what wisdom they would share with the world if they knew it was their last opportunity. Professor Randy Pausch, then a faculty member at Carnegie Mellon in Pittsburgh, Pennsylvania, accepted the challenge but learned soon thereafter that the pancreatic cancer that had been diagnosed a year earlier had metastasized and was terminal.

Although he initially hesitated over whether he would fulfill this commitment, because of Randy's yearning to find ways to ingeniously leave a legacy for his wife Jai and their three children, on September 18, 2007, he gave the lecture entitled "Really Achieving Your Childhood Dreams" to a standing room-only crowd. Perhaps the most meaningful point Randy made at the end of his lecture was when he stated: "It's not about how to achieve your dreams, it's how to lead your life. If you lead your life the right way, the karma will take care of itself, and the dreams will come to you." Sadly, Pausch died at the age of 47, just months after the book chronicling his life story and parting lecture, *The Last Lecture*, had been published. In so many ways, *GPS for Success* was written to fulfill his objectives, to enable the dreams of others and provide guidance about how to live your life.

DOI: 10.4324/9781003260387-17

ADDITIONAL INSPIRATIONAL STORIES/INSIGHTS

In closing, I'd like to conclude this self-help handbook with a potpourri of related topics, including unlooked-for opportunities, leadership and bringing out the best in those around you, avoiding overcautiousness, volunteering, reframing future commitments, the power of a thank you note, and giving back. We'll end the chapter with an anecdotal story regarding a major university commencement address I gave that yielded an unexpected surprise, a paragraph summary of the entire book, the enlightening excerpts from my favorite relevant poem, essentially a blueprint for life, and a parting challenge for you.

UNLOOKED-FOR OPPORTUNITIES

SOMETIMES OPPORTUNITY KNOCKS

Walter Lance, an American cartoonist, animator, and film producer, married actress Grace Stafford. During their honeymoon, he and Stafford kept hearing a woodpecker incessantly pecking on their cabin roof. Grace suggested that Walter use the bird for inspiration as a cartoon character. Initially a bit skeptical, he took her advice. Woody Woodpecker became an instant hit and got his own series the following year.

NAT KING COLE'S MARVELOUS VOICE: UNFORGETTABLE

Nat Cole was a piano player, working in small clubs wherever he could get bookings. One night, a customer who had had too much to drink noisily kept insisting that Nat sing a song while he was playing. Although Nat had never sung in public before, to avoid a scene, he gave it a shot. The rest is history—Nat "King" Cole had one of the most successful singing careers in modern show business.

LEADERSHIP: GREAT LEADERS ARE CATALYSTS

If your actions inspire others to dream more, learn more, do more, and become more, you're a leader.

John Quincy Adams

Ultimately, the only way to experience the richness of life is to live an attitude of gratitude: to appreciate what you have and what you can give. The best way to ensure your happiness is to assist others in experiencing their own.

Anthony Robbins

There is something that is much more scarce, something finer by far, something rarer than ability. It is the ability to recognize ability.

American writer, publisher, and philosopher Elbert Hubbard

You add value to people when you value them. It doesn't take much extra time or effort to be interested and demonstrate the value we have for others, especially those on whom we depend for mutual success.

John C. Maxwell

Numerous studies have shown that there are six especially important traits for leadership, and these include: *intelligence, confidence, charisma, determination, sociability,* and *integrity*. Moreover, great leaders invariably find positive purpose, ensure that their actions speak louder than their words, put people first, see an ocean of opportunities before them, and are great promoters. But there is one unparalleled test of leadership that is almost foolproof:

> When you can lead volunteers well, you can lead almost anyone.
>
> **John C. Maxwell**

It is largely for this reason that I've strongly advocated, throughout this book, joining and becoming active in professional organizations in your areas of interest, as these often serve as the ultimate leadership training laboratory and simultaneously allow you to expand your network of like-minded colleagues, including the "big names" in your field, in the United States and throughout the world.

Great leaders often take everybody on their staff/team up a notch or two. (Another reason why I say surround yourself with people who have skills, abilities, and resources you don't have—"hitch your wagon to a star.") One person, by virtue of his/her words, actions, and interactions, can bring out the best in all those around him/her. A great example of this is LeBron James, who in 2017 was identified by *Time Magazine* as one of the 100 Most Influential People in the World. Ironically, he was loudly criticized in the press in 2010 for leaving Cleveland to play for Miami in his quest to win another NBA championship. Yet, he ignited some mediocre players on both the Cleveland Cavaliers and Miami Heat and upped their games immensely. How? He was a team member, not the manager or coach. The answer? *By leading by example.* Because of his extraordinary skill set, physical attributes, tireless work ethic, great confidence, and leadership style, one that embraced *purpose-driven teamwork*, he inspired his teammates to perform to the highest levels possible, winning world championships in both cities. He further differentiated himself as a leader by generously giving back to the community and numerous worthy causes and charities throughout the nation.

AVOID OVERCAUTIOUSNESS—JUST DO IT!

Don't be overcautious. Bill Gates said, "To win big, you sometimes have to take big risks." Mark Cuban, Michael Jordan, Steve Jobs, Oprah Winfrey, Alice Walton, J.K. Rowling, and Warren Buffet, to name just a few, all took big risks. As the Nike commercial says, "Just Do It!" Sometimes, you just have to take risks when you're passionate about an innovative or pioneering idea that's counter to conventional wisdom or dogma. And, it's particularly challenging when all the naysayers around you emphatically state "it cannot be done" or "it's impossible." Ignore them! Especially if you've come up with a needed product or service for the masses. The late Zig Ziglar summed it up best: "You can get anything you want in life if you help enough other people get what they want."

Consider, for a moment, Mark Zuckerberg, an American internet entrepreneur and philanthropist who co-founded Facebook out of his college dorm room at Harvard and took the company public in May 2012. His pioneering ideas, which have influenced millions of people worldwide, have led to enormous wealth, making him worth approximately $101 billion today. Was Zuckerberg a risk taker? You bet!

During one interview, he offered the following excerpted insights for future entrepreneurs:

> The only strategy that's guaranteed to fail is not taking risks. You're not judged by your mistakes. I don't pretend that I had any idea what I was doing. I always felt like we were so close to dying in the first years, and we were afraid that Google was about to build our product and we were going to be screwed. You are going to make a ton of mistakes; you don't get judged by that. The biggest risk is not taking any risk. In a world that's changing really quickly, the only strategy that is guaranteed to fail is not taking risks.
>
> **Mark Zuckerberg**

TAKE RISKS: LEARN TO FAIL IF YOU WANT TO SUCCEED

Oftentimes, the only difference between failure and ultimate success is the determination to never give up. The greatest among us, that is, the highest achievers, are the ones who risked the most, tried the most often, and had the greatest number of setbacks or failures. We rarely remember or honor those who played it safe.

VOLUNTEER REQUESTED? RAISE YOUR HAND!

When we do more than we are paid to do, eventually we will be paid more for what we do.

Zig Ziglar

If I've learned anything about career advancement over the past four decades, when the boss or your supervisor requests a volunteer for a particular new program or initiative, raise your hand! This applies to association involvement as well. In corporations, people who routinely go above and beyond their specific job responsibilities (i.e., do more than they are paid to do) are invariably those who are among the first to be promoted. The same strategy holds for volunteers in professional associations—only these individuals advance to leadership roles.

The key is to complete your agreed-upon task in a timely and comprehensive manner, exceeding the requester's expectations (e.g., if a short [~2-page] report is requested within 2 weeks, submit a comprehensive well-written 4–5-page report within 1 week). In both the corporate and association worlds, management and leadership, respectively, have learned that "the past is prologue to the future." People who routinely exceed the decision-makers' expectations invariably ride the "magic carpet" to higher-level positions, prestige, salaries, benefits, and related perks. Looking for a career advancement secret weapon? Raise your hand high, quickly, and often when volunteers are requested, and follow through in an exemplary manner. Finally, don't talk or boast about the extra work you've done for the company you work for or the association you may be a member of. Your efforts will speak for themselves.☺

REFRAMING FUTURE COMMITMENTS: AVOID REGRET

As mentioned previously, integrity, that is, "doing what you say you're going to do," is a key characteristic of highly successful people and leaders in any field. Avoiding regret is another reason to follow through on verbal commitments. Alternatively, consider reframing future obligations that you may make, which may be forgotten or compromised by factors beyond your control.

Several years ago, I read a relevant story about an elderly Holocaust survivor, Sam, who was dying. His only living relative, a sister, summoned a rabbi to the hospital to meet with Sam to offer comfort. When leaving, the rabbi asked Sam if there was anything else he could do for him, or bring him, that might give him pleasure. Surprisingly, Sam replied that it would be great if the rabbi could bring him one of his favorite foods, a good piece of herring. The rabbi assured him he would be pleased to do so.

Granted, the life of a rabbi is demanding, being called on for countless joyous (e.g., bar mitzvahs, bat mitzvahs, weddings) and sorrowful occasions (e.g., funerals, hospital visits), as well as conducting Sabbath, weekly and holiday religious services, writing sermons, teaching, counseling, and invited presentations. A few days later, the rabbi received a call that Sam had died. When he and his wife paid a *shivah* (condolence) call, Sam's sister informed them that the last thing he said before he died was, "Do you think the rabbi will still bring me that piece of herring?"

The rabbi felt mortified by his slipped promise and wished he could turn the clock back. Although he sought forgiveness at Sam's funeral, his regrets lingered on—and a sobering lesson was learned. Even during our efforts to comfort others, our verbal commitments are indelible and may sometimes need to be reframed, especially when our follow-through may be distracted or compromised.

PROMISES MADE, PROMISES KEPT

Doing what you say you're going to do exemplifies integrity. The winners in life will go to great strides to fulfill what they commit to. Why? Because they said they would. Suggestion? *Write down all commitments that you make!* When you break a promise, the person you let down loses faith in you, and you lose faith in yourself, diminishing your self-esteem. To avoid breaking promises, learn to say "no" or "I'll try—but no guarantees" to commitments that you may have trouble keeping. Then, if you are, in fact, able to fulfill the request, you'll exceed their expectations and feel good about yourself.

THE POWER OF AN ACKNOWLEDGMENT NOTE

I got my first job out of college at a magazine because the hiring manager loved the Florentine paper that I used to write a thank you note so much that she actually kept my letter on her desk.

Lauren Young

Everyone has a basic need to know that he or she is making a difference. For those making a difference in your life, take the time to write them a note and express your appreciation for their relationship.

David Cottrell

According to one widely-cited study by Accountemps®, a staffing firm, approximately one in four job applicants send thank you notes after interviews—but 80 percent of hiring managers who receive them say they add insight and strength to the applicant's profile. I say, why stop there? Beyond the traditional, expected thank you note for a gift or especially kind gesture, there are powerful reasons for periodically sending an acknowledgment note to those friends, family, staff members, clients/ customers, and associates who make a difference in your life. This act alone provides a rapid and inexpensive way to strengthen relationships. It also keeps you focused on an "attitude of gratitude" and actively sets you apart in business and in life. Three tips in writing these notes: Write at unexpected times; make them as personalized as you can; and, keep them succinct (three to five sentences [maximum]), expressing your *sincere* appreciation and gratitude for the person or a deed they did (for you).

I also strongly believe that sending an acknowledgment note represents another way of sowing—an action that comes back to you in the future by reaping the associated rewards. Years ago, I got in the habit of reviewing nice things (e.g., speaking invitations, consulting, writing collaboration, or other opportunities) that came my way over the past year. For you, these may represent sales, business, or contracts. I invariably conducted this review between Thanksgiving and the first week of December, identifying those people who had done especially nice things or "opened doors for me" over the preceding months, and mailed a brief handwritten thank you note to each of them. Ironically, I began noticing that many of these same individuals came back to me the following year with similar and sometimes even greater opportunities. Perhaps it was the unexpected appreciation and gratitude that I expressed, the added visibility (i.e., visibility leads to opportunities [out of sight, out of mind]), the sowing analogy, or combinations thereof. Regardless, I came to understand the power of a year-end thank you or acknowledgment note as a forerunner to the holiday season and the New Year.

A related *Wall Street Journal* (*WSJ*) commentary (December 17, 2019) entitled "*A Thank-You Note Helped Me Find My Calling*, by Dr. Michael P.H. Stanley, a resident in neurology at the Massachusetts General Hospital, got my attention. During his middle school years, a reporter from a local newspaper interviewed him regarding his keyboard play during a series of concerts in the park. A friend of his father, Mr. Don Hardy, cut the interview out of the newspaper, laminated it, and mailed it to him. Michael asked his dad to tell Mr. Hardy "thank you" from him.

A few weeks later, Michael received a strange package in the mail that included an envelope, a stamp, a blank sheet of paper, and a golf pencil. What's this all about, Michael asked his father, who told him he'd have to figure it out on his own. Eventually, he realized that it was Mr. Hardy sending him a message—one that he has continued to practice to this day: *Always remember to write a thank you note.* Mr. Hardy, who had given his father advance warning of the lesson, stated that he thought Michael "might be destined for big things in a world where those little touches would make a difference, and so he wanted to fortify the habit of giving thanks."

Dr. Stanley, in this wonderful perspective, went on to note that when completing his answer to the residency applicant's question, he added that he was thankful that a small piece of paper could be used to convey heartfelt sentiments that have the power to change the lives of both sender and receiver. He concluded the *WSJ* commentary by reiterating that in our modern-day achievement culture, we must not forget that our merits derive in no small part from the support, advice, and counsel granted us by others. Sending a thank you or acknowledgement note is an act of not only gratitude but also humility and reminds us never to forget those who favorably influenced our destiny in life.

SERVICE PAYS DIVIDENDS: GIVE BACK!

A candle is not diminished by giving another candle light.

Earl Nightingale

Doing charitable or good things for other people will bring about a willingness and desire on their part to reciprocate in kind. There is nothing self-serving or manipulating about this—it's simply a matter of cause and effect. Like begets like. In relation to human behavior, it recognizes the natural inclination to reciprocity. People tend to reciprocate in the manner in which they are treated. When you perform a huge service to others, you will be paid huge dividends. There is no mystery about it, it's just so.

Helping others also has science-backed health and happiness benefits. People who volunteer, for example, tend to live longer, are less likely to become depressed later in life, and have better self-esteem. So, give back— to a cause, to a student or colleague, to a friend, even to a stranger.

Accordingly, I wasn't surprised when my research revealed that nearly all of the rich, famous, and super successful people that I've known or studied GIVE BACK, whether through donations/gifts, setting up charitable foundations, donating their time or expertise, favorably responding to requests (when possible), or helping or mentoring others. Such individuals realize that others helped them along the way—and, as alluded to earlier, are simply reciprocating in kind. They've also come to the realization that this gesture alone invariably leads to good karma. In essence, the domino effect of good luck or good fortune starts with you and invariably comes back to you. This preface leads me to a personal story I've told countless times over the years that has great relevance. I'd like to share it with you.

When I was an undergraduate student at Kent State University, we had an invited speaker one day, Dr. Herman K. Hellerstein, a world-renowned cardiologist who spoke on the value of regular exercise and preventive medicine. I had read several of his pioneering publications and was simply mesmerized by his presentation that day. A few weeks later, I decided to drive to the medical school where he served as Professor of Medicine, Case Western Reserve University, Cleveland, Ohio (my hometown), in the hope of sitting down with him to get some career advice. Unfortunately, I did not schedule an appointment. I entered his office and saw an elderly woman (his secretary) who looked a lot like the Wicked Witch of the West (Wizard of Oz). "Is Dr. Hellerstein in?" I asked. "Your name, please," she replied. "I'm Barry Franklin, a student at Kent State University, and I'm a big fan of Dr. Hellerstein," I responded. "Do you have an appointment?" she asked. "I don't, but really need only a few minutes of his time—and can certainly wait," I answered, now realizing that I hadn't gone about this in the manner I should have. She barked something along the lines of "Young man, you cannot see the Great and Powerful Wizard of Oz without an appointment!"

As I dejectedly left his office, heading back to Kent State University, I saw Dr. Hellerstein walking down the hall toward me and couldn't resist introducing myself. I mentioned that I was a big fan of his and that I had driven a long way to briefly meet with him, but that his secretary (Mrs. Husselman) said he was inundated with patients all day. "Come into my office," he replied. Several times during our meeting, Mrs. Husselman peeked into his office to tell him that patients were waiting—and to give me the "evil eye." *Long story short, Dr. Hellerstein spent more than an hour with me that day, and the inspirational meeting changed my life!* I now knew that I needed to pursue a PhD, and that I wanted to work in a clinical cardiology setting, with someone like him. I also vowed that if I ever became even modestly successful, I'd make the time to help students find their way, as he did for me—a complete stranger!

But the story isn't over yet. I went on to get my Master's degree and PhD from the University of Michigan and Penn State University, respectively, and 8 years later became a colleague of Dr. Hellerstein's, serving as Assistant Professor of Medicine at Case Western Reserve University, as a collaborating investigator on the National Exercise and Heart Disease Project. Surprising how things work out in life—or maybe not so surprising?! Ironically, I was now working my ass off—for him! Although he was a tough taskmaster, we published many papers together and remained good friends and colleagues until he passed. It was a great career opportunity! Indeed, he "opened many doors" for me. Looking back, it all started with a chance, unscheduled meeting years earlier where he made the time to help me identify a future career path. The lesson learned? Give back generously to others. Why? Because what goes around comes around.

MY COMMENCEMENT ADDRESS: AN UNEXPECTED SURPRISE

After I gave an invited presentation on leadership and keys to professional success at a student colloquium for a major, annual sports medicine meeting, a well-dressed middle-aged woman approached me and asked, "Dr. Franklin, can you give an abbreviated version of that talk as our upcoming commencement address?" I answered, "And you are?" She replied, "I'm Professor Charlotte (Toby) Tate, Dean at the University of Illinois, Chicago." My next question was the date and how many people would be in attendance. "There would be approximately 3,000 attendees, including our graduates and their families and friends, as well as our faculty," she replied. I looked at my calendar and said, "You can count on me." She went on, "You'll only have 10 minutes." I replied, "I'll make it work." She expanded the requisites: "You'll have to wear a cap and gown and all the commencement regalia." "No problem, thank you so very much for the invitation—I'm honored," I replied.

Now, in our family, my wife Linda is the business/financial person. I'd give away the farm. So, when I arrived home and excitedly told her about the invitation to speak at the commencement at the University of Illinois, Chicago, she asked, "Assuming your travel expenses are covered, what is the compensation or stipend that they are providing?" I said, "I didn't ask. It's an honor and a privilege to do a major university commencement address." She replied, "You're an idiot. People are always taking advantage of you." And I defensively responded, "I don't want to discuss this any further."

Two months before the commencement address, Dean Tate called me and said, "Barry, since you're coming to Chicago, do you want to bring your wife with you, on us?" I said to my wife, "Linda, they'll cover your airfare too, do you want to go?" She replied, "Of course, I'll go. It appears that's going to be your honorarium!" They put us up at a "five-star" hotel, and when we arrived, we were blown away by the amenities. On top of that, there were a half-dozen roses in the luxurious hotel suite with a note to my wife Linda, "Thanks for sharing Barry with us. From, Dean Tate, on behalf of the College of Health Sciences." Unbelievable! The Dean took us out to a great dinner the evening before the commencement, and I was very pleased that my 10-minute presentation was so well received the following day.

As we were flying back home, my wife said, "This was very nice, but I still say you should have been paid for your inspirational commencement address." I replied, "Look, I don't want to discuss this anymore. It's a big deal to be asked to deliver a major university commencement address—and we were treated like royalty. Let's let it go." Three weeks later, I called my wife, which I often do over the noon hour, to see what was going on. "Oh, I'm just bringing the mail in. There's a letter from the Dean's office at the University of Illinois." I replied, "Open it up. It's probably a thank you note." All of a sudden, there's silence ... *absolute silence* at the other end of the phone. I asked, "Linda, are you still there? Did we get cut off? Lin?"

"Dean Tate is my new best friend," she sheepishly uttered. "There's a thank you note enclosed, but there's also a check for $3,000. Did you know that?" I replied, "No, I didn't." And, that's the point! In life, if it's potentially beneficial for you, do what YOU want to do. Your participation should not be predicated on whether you are offered a generous stipend or not. On countless occasions, I've given invited presentations for little or no remuneration, only to have someone in the audience subsequently contact me regarding speaking at a generously compensated event for them, oftentimes in a fun or exotic location. As I've said before, *visibility leads to opportunities*. Do things right for people, try to exceed their expectations, and good things will happen to you. Admittedly, it won't always be a $3,000 unexpected check.☺

THE CONDENSED "FRANKLIN GPS FOR SUCCESS" FORMULA

Building a highly successful career involves investing time, effort, and hard work into things that matter ….

Both satisfaction and benefaction derive from attitude and action: Love what you do; take 100 percent responsibility for your life; focus on your contributions rather than the rewards; look for the *good* in people and situations; write down and constantly think about your goals; abandon perceived limits; find "stars" as early career mentors and associates; get involved in professional associations (adopt a greater cause); serve others—make everyone you meet feel important; don't tell people, show them; take action; smile more; recognize that setbacks line the road to success, and that persistence pays; put people first and treat them as you'd want to be treated; partner with others who have skills, abilities, or resources you don't have; exemplify *integrity*; prepare for success (10,000-hour rule); go for the gold; routinely exceed people's expectations; see an ocean of opportunities before you; strive for constant improvement; become a promoter (visibility = opportunities); raise your hand when volunteers are requested; and, give back generously. Avoid the deceiving "instant gratification" that comes from saying something nasty, potentially offensive, or disrespectful to others. By doing so, you irreparably lock doors of opportunity that could have been opened for you by those with whom you've had a falling out. Silence is golden! Finally, hang around people who are smarter than you are and far more accomplished in the field(s) that you wish to pursue. You'll find that the lessons learned and the opportunities that will arise will be priceless. ☺

My favorite relevant poem, shown here, provides a *blueprint* for leading your life in the right way—the forerunner of future happiness and overwhelming success.

"What Will Matter" by Michael Josephson*
Ready or not, some day it will all come to an end.
There will be no more sunrises, no minutes, hours or days.
All the things you collected, whether treasured or forgotten
    will pass to someone else.
Your wealth, fame and temporal power will shrivel to
    irrelevance.
It will not matter what you owned or what you were owed.
Your grudges, resentments, frustrations and jealousies will
    finally disappear.
So too, your hopes, ambitions, plans and to do lists will expire.
The wins and losses that once seemed so important will fade
    away.
It won't matter where you came from or what side of the tracks
    you lived on at the end.
It won't matter whether you were beautiful or brilliant.
Even your gender and skin color will be irrelevant.
So what will matter? How will the value of your days be
    measured?
What will matter is not what you bought but what you built,
    not what you got but what you gave.
What will matter is not your success but your significance.
What will matter is not what you learned but what you taught.
What will matter is every act of integrity, compassion, courage,
    or sacrifice that enriched, empowered or encouraged others to
    emulate your example.
What will matter is not your competence but your character.
What will matter is not how many people you knew, but how
    many will feel a lasting loss when you're gone.
What will matter is not your memories, but the memories of
    those who loved you.
What will matter is how long you will be remembered, by
    whom and for what.
Living a life that matters doesn't happen by accident.

It's not a matter of circumstance but of choice.
Choose to live a life that matters.

A PARTING CHALLENGE FOR YOU

Perhaps Henry David Thoreau summed it up best when he said: "If one advances confidently in the direction of his dreams, and endeavors to live the life which he has imagined, he will meet with a success unexpected in common hours."

The truth most of us miss in this enduring quotation is that success lies in wait for those who bring it to fruition. The skills, strategies, and secrets in this book will motivate, inspire, and empower you to do just that. You've got everything you need to live the life that you've imagined. If these worked for me, and countless others, they'll work for you. Read and reread this book, underline or highlight key points, and most importantly, assimilate, embrace, and regularly *apply* what you learn in your everyday life. By following these recommendations, "good luck" will be increasingly attracted to you. It will happen! Don't be surprised. Believe, act, and achieve. Nothing can stop you—but yourself.

In closing, let's bring it all back to the film clip from *Dead Poet's Society* and the watch words of schoolteacher John Keating: "Carpe diem. Seize the day. Make your lives extraordinary."

THE END (but for you, it's only the beginning). Godspeed!

Epilogue: Early on, the late basketball superstar Kobe Bryant came to the realization that you alone have the single greatest impact on how to lead your life and find the work that you love. Accordingly, he promulgated the notion that there's only one "sure thing" in life. "If you're going to bet on someone, bet on yourself," Bryant contended.

Section IV

Appendices

Appendix A: Memorable Success Quotes

(Expressing) appreciation can make a day, even change a life. Your willingness to put it into words is all that is necessary.

Margaret Cousins

Write it down. Written goals have a way of transforming wishes into wants; cant's into cans; dreams into plans; and plans into reality. Don't just think it—ink it!

Unknown Author

You have to put in many, many, many tiny efforts that nobody sees or appreciates before you achieve anything worthwhile.

Brian Tracy

Don't spend your precious time asking, "why isn't the world a better place?" It will only be time wasted. The question to ask is "How can I make it better?" To that there is an answer.

Leo Buscaglia

Only through focus can you do world-class things, no matter how capable you are.

Bill Gates

Example is not the main thing in influencing others, it is the only thing.

Albert Schweitzer

No act of kindness, no matter how small is ever wasted.

Aesop

A real decision is measured by the fact that you've taken a new action. If there's no action, you haven't truly decided.

Tony Robbins

DOI: 10.4324/9781003260387-19

There is a real magic in enthusiasm. It spells the difference between mediocrity and accomplishment.

Norman Vincent Peale

Life is not measured by the number of breaths we take, but by the moments that take our breath away.

George Carlin

As we express our gratitude, we must never forget that the highest appreciation is not to utter words, but to live by them.

John F. Kennedy

Develop success from failures. Discouragement and failure are two of the surest stepping stones to success.

Dale Carnegie

Attitudes are contagious. Is yours worth catching?

Dennis Mannering

Strive to be first: first to smile, first to say hello, first to compliment, and first to forgive.

Unknown Author

What would you attempt to do if you knew you would not fail?

Robert Schuller

Sometimes you get your greatest direction from your greatest rejection.

T.D. Jakes

Life is a risk—you can't steal second base and keep your foot on first.

Unknown Author

Think little goals and expect little achievements. Think big goals and win big success.

David Schwartz

Most of our obstacles would melt away if, instead of cowering before them, we should walk boldly through them.

Orison Marden

I know the price of success: dedication, hard work, and an unremitting devotion to the things you want to see happen.

Frank Lloyd Wright

In the middle of every difficulty lies opportunity.

Albert Einstein

Once you choose hope, anything's possible.

Christopher Reeve

I'm a great believer in luck, and I find the harder I work, the more luck I have.

Thomas Jefferson

Real integrity is doing the right thing, knowing that nobody's going to know whether you did or not.

Oprah Winfrey

Don't look down on someone unless you are helping them up.

Unknown Author

The best way to cheer yourself up is to try to cheer somebody else up.

Mark Twain

People with goals succeed because they know where they are going.

Earl Nightingale

It's always too early to quit.

Norman Vincent Peale

The difference between try and triumph is a little umph!

Unknown Author

Discipline is the bridge between goals and accomplishments.

Jim Rohn

People become really quite remarkable when they start thinking they can do things. When they believe in themselves, they have the first secret of success.

Norman Vincent Peale

The best way to make your dreams come true is to wake up.

Paul Valery

Those who bring sunshine into the lives of others cannot keep it from themselves.

James Barrie

When one door of happiness closes, another one opens but often we look so long at the closed door that we do not see the one which has opened for us.

Helen Keller

The elevator to success is out of order. You have to use the stairs ... one step at a time.

Joe Girard

Greatness is not defined by what a person receives, but by what a person gives.

Unknown Author

Don't count the days, make each day count.

Unknown Author

When you forgive, you in no way change the past—but you sure do change the future.

Bernard Meltzer

Don't be afraid to take a chance ... remember, the greatest failure is to not try.

Debbi Fields (founder of Mrs. Field's Cookies)

Patience, persistence and perspiration make an unbeatable combination for success.

Napoleon Hill

It is one of the most beautiful compensations of life, that no man can sincerely try to help another without helping himself.

Ralph Waldo Emerson

The only people you should ever get "EVEN" with are those who have helped you.

John Honeyfeld

Treat everyone you meet as though they are the most important person you'll meet that day.

Roger Dawson

Success means having the courage, the determination, and the will to become the person you believe you were meant to be.

George Sheehan

If your ship doesn't come in, swim out to it.

Jonathan Winters

Being defeated is often only a temporary condition. Giving up is what makes it permanent.

Marilyn vos Savant

When you get into a tight place and everything goes against you, till it seems as though you could not hold on a minute longer, never give up then—for that is just the time and place the tide will turn.

Harriet Beecher Stowe

The door to opportunity is always labeled "push."

Unknown Author

Avoiding the phrase, "*I don't have time ...*" will soon help you to realize that you do have the time needed for just about anything you choose to accomplish in life.

Bo Bennett

The greatest discovery of my generation is that a man can alter his life simply by altering his attitude of mind.

John Adams

A warm smile is the universal language of kindness.

William Ward

Most of the important things in the world have been accomplished by people who have kept on trying when there seemed to be no hope at all.

Dale Carnegie

If opportunity doesn't knock, build a door.

Milton Berle

Kind words may be short, but their echoes are endless.

Mother Teresa

Every day is a new opportunity. You can build on yesterday's success or put its failures behind and start over again. That's the way life is, with a new game every day, and that's the way baseball is.

Bob Feller

If you are going to achieve excellence in big things, you develop the habit in little matters. Excellence is not an exception, it is a prevailing attitude.

Colin Powell

Success is not the key to happiness. Happiness is the key to success. If you love what you are doing, you will be successful.

Herman Cain

Success seems to be largely a matter of hanging on after others have let go.

William Feather

Whenever you see a successful person, you only see the public glories, never the private sacrifices to reach them.

Vaibhav Shah

Opportunities don't happen. You create them.

Chris Grosser

The best revenge is massive success.

Frank Sinatra

I have not failed. I've just found 10,000 ways that won't work.

Thomas Edison

What seems to us as bitter trials are often blessings in disguise.

Oscar Wilde

There are two types of people who will tell you that you cannot make a difference in this world: those who are afraid to try and those who are afraid you will succeed.

Ray Goforth

The starting point of all achievement is desire.

Napoleon Hill

Success is the sum of small efforts, repeated day-in and day-out.

Robert Collier

We become what we think about most of the time, and that's the strangest secret.

Earl Nightingale

Twenty years from now you will be more disappointed by the things that you didn't do than by the ones you did do. So throw off the bowlines. Sail away from the safe harbor. Catch the trade winds in your sails. Explore. Dream. Discover.

Mark Twain

Rarely have I seen a situation where doing less than the other guy is a good strategy.

Jimmy Spithill

Success does not consist in never making mistakes but in never making the same one a second time.

George Bernard Shaw

Nobody ever wrote down a plan to be broke, fat, lazy, or stupid. Those things are what happen when you don't have a plan.

Larry Winget

Be content to act, and leave the talking to others.

Baltasar Gracian

Many of life's failures are people who did not realize how close they were to success when they gave up.

Thomas A. Edison

Would you like me to give you a formula for success? It's quite simple, really: Double your rate of failure. You are thinking of failure as the enemy of success. But it isn't at all. You can be discouraged by failure or you can learn from it, so go ahead and make mistakes. Make all you can. Because remember that's where you will find success.

Thomas J. Watson

Logic will get you from A to B. Imagination will take you everywhere.

Albert Einstein

Success is just a war of attrition. Sure, there's an element of talent you should probably possess. But if you just stick around long enough, eventually something is going to happen.

Dax Shepard

If there is something to gain and nothing to lose by asking, by all means ask!

W. Clement Stone

If you don't ask, you don't get.

Gandhi

The greatest good we can do for others is not to share our riches but to reveal theirs.

Unknown Author

You create your opportunities by asking for them.

Patty Hansen

A committee of three gets things done if two don't show up.

Herbert V. Prochnow

No one ever attains very eminent success by simply doing what is required of him; it is the amount and excellence of what is over and above the required, that determines the greatness of ultimate distinction.

Charles Kendall Adams

Luck is a dividend of sweat. The more you sweat the luckier you get.

Ray Kroc

Any definition of a successful life must include serving others.

George Bush

It takes a person with a mission to succeed.

Clarence Thomas

You don't always get what you ask for, but you never get what you don't ask for ... unless it's contagious!

Franklin Broude

It takes twenty years to make an overnight success.

Eddie Cantor

To be successful, the first thing to do is fall in love with your work.

Sister Mary Lauretta

Even when I went to the playground, I never picked the best players. I picked the guys with less talent, but who were willing to work hard ... and put in the effort, who had the desire to be great.

Earvin "Magic" Johnson

Success is a state of mind. If you want success, start thinking of yourself as a success.

Joyce Brothers

As I grow older, I pay less attention to what men say. I just watch what men do.

Andrew Carnegie

People succeed because they believe, not only that they can and will succeed, but also that success is worth the price they pay for it.

Tom Hopkins

If you could get the courage to begin, you have the courage to succeed.

David Viscott

Always do your best. What you plant now, you will harvest later.

Og Mandino

The best career advice to give the young is, "Find out what you like doing best and get someone to pay you for doing it."

Katherine Whitehorn

The object of business is not to make others comfortable, but to make them successful.

Laurel Cutler

Actually, all I ever wanted to be was the best in my field.

Lou Holtz

I am not judged by the number of times I fail, but by the number of times I succeed; and the number of times I succeed is in direct proportion to the number of times I can fail and keep on trying.

Tom Hopkins

The key to getting everything you want is to never put all your begs into one ask-it!

Unknown Author

Success is not achieved by working until the whistle sounds at the end of the day but by working even though the whistle has sounded at the end of the day.

Roderick Van Murchison

Life's garden is filled with seeds of success. Failures are simple fertilizer for the soil.

Monica Kazmier

You don't start climbing a mountain to get to the middle. Why be content with being average?

James Hart

You wouldn't worry so much about what others think of you if you realized how seldom they do.

Eleanor Roosevelt

Three things in human life are important. The first is to be kind. The second is to be kind. And the third is to be kind.

Henry James

Don't wait. The time will never be just right.

Napoleon Hill

The ground work for all happiness is health.

James Leigh Hunt

Life isn't about getting and having—it's about giving and being.

Kevin Kruse

Life has 2 rules: #1, never quit. #2, always remember rule #1.

Duke Ellington

I've had a lot of worries in my life—most of which never happened.

Mark Twain

You can make mistakes, but you aren't a failure until you start blaming others for those mistakes.

John Wooden

Continually bombard your mind with thoughts, words, pictures, and people consistent with the person you want to be and the goals you want to achieve.

Brian Tracy

Think in negative terms, get negative results. Think in positive terms, you will achieve positive results.

Norman Vincent Peale

In order to get what you've never had, you must be willing to do what you've never done.

Rev. Edgar Vann

Kindness is the language which the deaf can hear and the blind can see.

Mark Twain

You can accomplish by kindness what you cannot by force.

Publilius Syrus

The greatest pleasure in life is doing what people say you cannot do.

Walter Bagehot

If you only do what you know you can do—you never do very much.

Tom Krause

A fool with a plan can outsmart a genius with no plan.

T. Boone Pickens

I learned so much, so very much about myself in defeat. I've learned very little to nothing in victory.

Floyd Patterson

Obstacles are things a person sees when he takes his eyes off his/her goal.

E. Joseph Cossman

It is our choices ... that show what we truly are, far more than our abilities.

J.K. Rowling

If you'll not settle for anything less than your best, you'll be amazed at what you can accomplish in your lives.

Legendary football coach Vince Lombardi

Fortune favors the brave.

Roman author, Gaius Plinius Secundus

Perpetual optimism is a force multiplier.

Colin Powell

Service to others is the rent you pay for your room here on earth.

Muhammad Ali (originally by Emma Vernon)

The ladder of success works like any other ladder. Very few have climbed it with their hands in their pockets.

Zig Ziglar

You get better results if you have high expectations. This is true in science, math, reading, football, or band.

Charles Adair

The secret of getting ahead is getting started.

Zig Ziglar

Appendix B: Additional Success Resources

Lead the Field by Earl Nightingale, Nightingale-Conant Corporation, Niles, Illinois.

TNT: The Power Within You by Claude M. Bristol and Harold Sherman, Fireside, New York, New York, 1992.

TNT: It Rocks the Earth by Claude M. Bristol, BN Publishing, 2007.

The Ultimate Success Secret by Daniel S. Kennedy, Kimble and Kennedy Publishing, Austin, Texas, 2004.

Being Happy! A Handbook to Greater Confidence & Security by Andrew Matthews, Price Stern Sloan, Inc., Los Angeles, California, 1990.

Smile & Succeed for Teens by Kirk Manecke, Solid Press, LLC, Milford, Michigan, 2014.

The Essence of Success by Earl Nightingale, Nightingale-Conant Corporation, 1993.

The Success Principles by Jack Canfield with Janet Switzer, Harper Collins Publishers, Inc., New York, New York, 2005.

The Prayer of Jabez by Bruce Wilkinson with David Kopp, Multnomah Books, Colorado Springs, Colorado, 2000.

Having It All by John Assaraf, Atria Books, New York, New York, 2003.

The Fred Factor by Mark Sanborn, Doubleday, New York, New York, 2004.

Notes from a Friend by Anthony Robbins, Fireside, New York, New York, 1995.

Success 101: What Every Leader Needs to Know by John C. Maxwell, Thomas Nelson, Nashville, Tennessee, 2008.

How to Sell Anything to Anybody by Joe Girard with Stanley H. Brown, Fireside, New York, New York, 2006.

The 80/20 Principle by Richard Koch, Doubleday, New York, New York, 1998.

Yes You Can by Jack Collins, Harper Collins Publisher, Sydney, Australia, 1997.

The Magic of Believing by Claude M. Bristol, Fireside, New York, New York, 1985.

No B.S.: Time Management for Entrepreneurs by Dan Kennedy, Entrepreneur Press, Vancouver, Canada, 2004.

Ask More, Get More by Michael Alden, Emerald Book Company, Austin, Texas, 2014.

The Strangest Secret by Earl Nightingale, BN Publishing, 2006.

The Secret by Rhonda Byrne, Atria Books, New York, New York, 2006.

Focus on the Good Stuff: The Power of Appreciation by Mike Robbins, John Wiley & Sons (Jossey-Bass), San Francisco, California, 2007.

How Full Is Your Bucket? by Tom Rath and Donald O. Clifton, Gallup Press, New York, New York, 2004.

How to Make Luck: Seven Secrets Lucky People Use to Succeed by Marc Myers, Renaissance Books, United Kingdom, 1998.

Outliers: The Story of Success by Malcolm Gladwell, Little, Brown and Company, New York, New York, 2008.

Rudy's Rules for Success by Rudy Ruettiger and Mike Celizic, Doddridge Press, Dallas, Texas, 1995.

The Original Think and Grow Rich by Napoleon Hills, Summit Publishing, Brighton, Michigan, 2008 (this book is a reprint of the original version published in 1937).

Aspire: 3 Powerful Strategies for Creating More of What You Want, Now by Ole Carlson, Greenleaf Book Group, Seattle, Washington, 2009.

I Can See You Naked by Ron Hoff, Andrews and McMeel, Kansas City, Missouri, 1988.

Speak with Confidence by Dianna Booher, McGraw-Hill, New York, New York, 2003.

Believe You Can: The Power of a Positive Attitude by John Mason, Revell (Spire), Grand Rapids, Michigan, 2004.

The Leader in You by Dale Carnegie and associates, Pocket Books, New York, New York, 1993.

The 24-Hour Turn-Around by Jim Hartness and Neil Eskelin, Revell (Spire), Grand Rapids, Michigan, 2002.

Don't Sweat the Small Stuff ... and It's All Small Stuff by Richard Carlson, Hyperion, New York, New York, 1997.

If Success Is a Game, These Are the Rules by Chérie Carter Scott, Broadway Books, New York, New York, 2000.

Doing It Now by Edwin C. Bliss, Bantam Books, New York, New York, 1986.

Tin Cup Dreams: A Long Shot Makes It on the PGA Tour by Michael D'Antonio, Hyperion Press, New York, New York, 2000.

Happiness by Matthieu Ricard, Little, Brown and Company, New York, New York, 2003.

Shift Happens! Powerful Ways to Transform Your Life by Robert Holden, Jeffers Press, Santa Monica, California, 2000.

Success Secrets: A Common Sense Guide to Lifelong Achievement by Merrill Douglass, Honor Books, Tulsa, Oklahoma, 1984.

Napoleon Hill's Keys to Success edited by Matthew Sartwell, Plume, New York, New York, 1997.

The 100 Simple Secrets of Successful People by David Niven, Harper Collins Publishers, New York, New York, 2002.

Bringing Out the Best in People by Alan Loy McGinnis, Augsburg Publishing House, Minneapolis, Minnesota, 1985.

How to Win Friends & Influence People by Dale Carnegie, Pocket Books, New York, New York, 1981 (revised edition).

Top Performance: How to Develop Excellence in Yourself and Others by Zig Ziglar, Berkley Books, New York, New York, 1986.

The Ten Commandments of Success by James A. Belasco, New Millennium Press, Beverly Hills, California, 2000.

The 21 Indispensable Qualities of a Leader by John C. Maxwell, Thomas Nelson Publishers, Nashville, Tennessee, 1999.

The One Thing You Need to Know by Marcus Buckingham, Free Press, New York, New York, 2005.

Skills for Life: The Fundamentals You Need to Succeed by Mike Jarvis and Jonathan Peck, Skills for Life, LLC, New York, New York, 2003.

A Strategy for Winning by Carl Mays, Lincoln-Bradley Publishing, New York, New York, 1991.

Success Is a Choice: Ten Steps to Overachieving in Business and Life by Rick Pitino with Bill Reynolds, Broadway Books, New York, New York, 1997.

Create Your Own Luck: 8 Principles of Attracting Good Fortune in Life, Love, and Work by Azriela Jaffe, Adams Media Corporation, Holbrook, Massachusetts, 2000.

Unstoppable by Cynthia Kersey, Sourcebooks, Inc., Naperville, Illinois, 1998.

Developing the Leader Within You by John C. Maxwell, Thomas Nelson Publishers, Nashville, Tennessee, 1993.

The Agile Manager's Guide to Goal-Setting and Achievement by Walter J. Wadsworth, Velocity Business Publishing, Bristol, Vermont, 1998.

The Eagle's Secret: Success Strategies for Thriving at Work & in Life by David McNally, Dell Publishing, New York, New York, 1998.

You Can Reach the Top by Zig Ziglar, River Oak Publishing, Tulsa, Oklahoma, 2001.

The Purpose Driven Life by Rick Warren, Zondervan, Grand Rapids, Michigan, 2002.

Believe and Achieve! by Paul Hanna, Penguin Books, Ringwood, Victoria, Australia, 1998.

Little Gold Book of Yes! Attitude by Jeffrey Gitomer, FT Press, Upper Saddle River, New Jersey, 2007.

The Magic Lamp: Goal Setting for People Who Hate Setting Goals by Keith Ellis, Three Rivers Press, New York, New York, 1996.

Dare to Win by Jack Canfield and Mark Victor Hansen, Berkley Books, New York, New York, 1994.

The Magic of Thinking Big by David J. Schwartz, Fireside (Simon & Schuster), New York, New York, 1987.

Simple Steps to Impossible Dreams by Steven K. Scott, Fireside (Simon & Schuster), New York, New York, 1998.

You Can Do It! by Paul Hanna, Penguin Books, Ringwood, Victoria, Australia, 1997.

The Aladdin Factor by Jack Canfield and Mark Victor Hansen, Berkley Books, New York, New York, 1995.

Yes, You Can! by Sam Deep and Lyle Sussman, Perseus Books, Reading, Massachusetts, 1996.

Second Thoughts by Mort Crim, Health Communications, Inc., Deerfield Beach, Florida, 1997.

The Winner Within by Pat Riley, Berkley Books, New York, New York, 1993.

Good to Great by Jim Collins, Harper Collins Publishers, Inc., New York, New York, 2001.

All You Can Do Is All You Can Do But All You Can Do Is Enough! by A.L. Williams, Thomas Nelson Incorporated, Nashville, Tennessee, 1988.

Secrets of Mind Power by Harry Lorayne, Lifetime Books, Inc., Hollywood, Florida, 1995.

A Touch of Wonder by Arthur Gordon, Jove (Glass Frog Books), Hawthorne, California, 1986.

Dare to Be Great: The Unauthorized Story of Glenn Turner by Rudy Maxa, Morrow Publishing Company, New York, 1977.

Mind Hacking: How to Change Your Mind for Good in 21 Days by Sir John Hargrave, Simon and Schuster, New York, 2017.

The Power of Your Subconscious Mind by Joseph Murphy, Penguin Books, New York, 2009.

The Curmudgeon's Guide to Getting Ahead: Dos and Don'ts of Right Behavior, Tough Thinking, Clear Writing, and Living a Good Life by Charles Murray, Currency Press, Redfern, New South Wales, Australia, 2014.

Peak: Secrets from the New Science of Expertise by K. Anders Ericsson and Robert Pool, Eamon Dolan/Houghton Mifflin Harcourt, Boston, Massachusetts, 2017.

Official Guide to Success by Tom Hopkins, Harper Collins Publishers, New York, 1985 (original edition).

The Science of Success: What Researchers Know That You Should Know by Paula J. Caproni, Van Rye Publishing, LLC, Ann Arbor, Michigan, 2017.

Do the Right Thing, Do It All the Time: 75 Success Secrets Listed for Fast Reference by Frank Leigh, Can and Will Books, 2018.

Index